"As a small business owner I was always thinking next year would even be better. I could stop living from day to day. I had always made good money, just not enough to live the way I wanted to and still invest in my future. So after changing to Tom's CPA firm, I started taking the steps that he outlined for me to successfully sell my business and retire. Follow Tom's guidelines and you will be successful in retiring and/or your exit planning. This book will take you from where you are to where you want to be."

—Gary Price, Former Owner of Western States Steel, Inc.,
Spokane, Washington

"A few weeks ago we sold our business after having Tom Griffiths coach us closely for two years, and as a result we read this book with great interest. Tom is a master at being "The Missing Advisor", and his book gives you a taste of what it is like to work with him! He has an ability to see and communicate the big picture and yet give you the "next step" (something that often seemed elusive to us). His practical suggestions were absolutely invaluable. Reading this book was like reviewing our past two years of work with him. So, whether you are establishing a business, managing one, or getting ready to sell it, this book is a treasure!"

—Len and Ruth Harms, Founders and Former Owners of
Harms Engineering, Inc., Tri-Cities, Washington

"In truth, most business owners don't treat their business as an investment! From real life experiences working with main street business owners, Tom Griffiths offers a refreshingly new practical guidebook to build a management program for the life of your business. A must read for small business owners who want a legacy—joining The 2% Club."

—Ted W. Schinzel, SBA Area Manager, Spokane, Washington

"Small business owners are completely invested in their business however most don't have a game plan for maximizing their success. Most don't realize what type of impact such a plan can have not only on their financial success but their overall quality of life as well. This step by step process built around the five rules for success will put business owners young and old, large and small, light years closer to achieving the dream that put them in business to begin with. His book is a must read for any business owner and should be handed out by every chamber of commerce in America!"

—Bill Parsons, CPA, PFS, Owner,
Mainsail Asset Management, Scottsboro, Alabama

"Want to join The 2% Club? So did I, but just couldn't find the expertise.....until I met Tom Griffiths, CPA. Tom took me through The 2% Club Roadmap for Success step by step. Results happen, I am a believer! I passionately recommend Tom Griffiths and The 2% Club."

—Ricky Grunden, Sr., President & CEO,
Grunden Financial Advisory, Inc., Denton, Texas

The 10 Steps of Successful Small Business Owners

The 10 Steps of Successful Small Business Owners

Your Roadmap for Joining The 2% Club

Thomas M. Griffiths

To my wife

Roxanne

Your love and support
are the foundation
of my life.

Contents

CHAPTER 1

The Missing Advisor

In business, as in life, there are no certainties. That's something that I experienced firsthand not too long ago—an experience that would ultimately change my life, and one that I've used to help change the lives of my clients.

In 2000, I was heading up a very successful CPA firm—my own business. I was thirty-five years old and had just started a family; my wife and I had two beautiful children, a son and a daughter. It was an uphill climb, and not in the bad sense: I could see the horizons in front of me, and they were bright, full of promise.

Then, one day, sitting in my doctor's office, I was thrown for a loop. In for a checkup, I was waiting on the table, legs dangling off the side, watching the clock slowly tick forward and thinking of the meetings I had to get to and the clients I'd need to see that afternoon. The doctor wheeled in with a concerned look on his face. "Tom," he said, "there are some spots on this chest x-ray we took. We need to send you to a specialist to get this checked out."

It's one of those moments that make you feel like you're shrinking down to nothing, and the world in front of you has just gotten unmanageably large. Suddenly, I couldn't see the horizon anymore; I could barely see the hand in front of my face.

I went home from the appointment to tell my wife what the doctor had said, and made arrangements to go see the specialist that my doctor recommended. While I waited to find out exactly what I would be facing, my mind swirled with questions. What will happen to my business if I die? Who would buy it? How will my wife get paid a fair value for all that I've worked to build? Would that value be enough to provide for my family? … see my two small children through their lives ahead? … put food on the table? Simply put, I had no idea what I was dealing with—not just about my health, but also about the viability of my family's future. And it wasn't for lack of effort, either. I had been successful in my business because I had the drive, the acumen, and the sense to be forward-thinking, but I was in the midst of a humbling experience, one that taught me that sometimes all the hard work in the world won't help you when life throws you these kinds of curves.

When I sat down to take a hard look at these questions and search for any possible answers, I found that a lot of my sounding boards were saying the same thing: "You're good with money, right? Shouldn't you be able to figure something out?"

It was true; my background was as a CPA. But these were not tax and accounting questions—these were entirely different quandaries: financial planning questions. Like most people, I thought my investment advisor could help me with my financial challenges; after all, financial advising is the role of a financial advisor. But I was disappointed to find out that while he selected funds in which to place my investments, most of his clients were not business owners, and as such, he offered no expertise in solving my financial challenges.

Thankfully, my medical situation turned out to be manageable. I spent five years working with the specialist to develop a solution that would stop the progression of my lung disease. While my health situation was slowly improving, I was able to take a hard look at my questions and develop the resolve to create my own answers. That's when I decided I wanted to become the best advisor I could be for the small business owner, an advisor who could solve those particular needs that fall through the cracks that exist between the advice of their CPAs and that of their financial advisors. My personal health scare had taught me that those two voices simply aren't enough, that the small business owner is missing a key advisor, one who bridges the gap between business and personal advice. So I set out on my journey to become "The Missing Advisor." One of the first things I discovered on my journey was that only 2% of small business owners were solving the puzzle and finding their way to success. I call this very rare but highly successful group The 2% Club, and I have written this book to help you become a member.

This is where my story ends, and yours begins. Let's write it together.

CHAPTER 2

Meet The 2% Club

When I first set about preparing my firm to help Main Street business owners become financially successful, I knew that I could learn valuable lessons by researching what already-successful business minds had done to get to the top. I logged hundreds of hours and several years interviewing these success stories: men and women who have a net worth between $1-10 million, with assets under management in their investment portfolios of about $300,000 to $3 million. Other than their investments and their property holdings, they all had one big thing in common: their business represented a significant portion of their assets, their net worth, and thus, their prospects for their (and their family's) future.

These men and women came from diverse backgrounds and had built companies that served diverse needs. But more and more, I was noticing commonalities that drove their success. These commonalities would eventually become the framework for the **Five Rules of The 2% Club,** which we'll unpack later on in this book.

Another, more insidious commonality made itself known shortly into my research—one that belonged not to the successful models but to the unfortunate and ever-growing tally of failures that dotted the landscape of Main Street.

Again and again, it became obvious to me that only 2% of these business owners could be considered successful. The other 98% were succumbing to various challenges, chief among them were disease, death, divorce, but mostly distressed business models. Having danced with my own "D-word" devil, it really hit home for me how thin and delicate the line separating a successful business from a bankruptcy filing could be. With no disrespect intended to these industrious individuals or their financial advisors and CPAs, they fell victim to the one-two punch of a lack of appropriate advice for their individual situations (as we've said before, these business owners need more than just tax and investment planning) and those dark demons that no one can fully control. The problem with all those "D-words" is that once they've started to set in, the damage has already been done. Just as there is only so much a doctor can do after a tumor has metastasized, there is not much that can be done to control events that are already set in motion, snowballing out of control in a business owner's life, his or her bank account, and his or her bottom line. In these cases, prevention is the cure that would have helped them, had they been able to put it in place soon enough.

Here are some other (unpleasant—sorry!) facts for you to consider:

> › 40% of new businesses fail during their first year.

> › 80% of businesses fail within five years.

> › 96% of businesses fail within the first ten years.

> › Of those remaining 4% still in business after ten years, only half of those business owners (2%—sound familiar?) are able to leave their businesses when they want to, on their own terms, and with something to retire on.

While it was too late for those 98% that I was researching, I gained immense hope as I studied the commonalities within The 2% Club. That club is made up of those who *were* successful—those who were implementing the same preventative and planning-oriented rules time after time. And the club's membership rolls are always open.

Now I've been able to put into practice what I've learned from all that research. My firm is entirely devoted to breaking down those common rules, innovating practical solutions, and helping clients implement strategies that follow the Five Rules so that they, too, may overcome these challenges and join in the ranks of The 2% Club.

Another piece of good news that I've gleaned from this process is something I'm more than happy to pass on to you before we go too much further—if you're eyeing that top echelon, thinking that you have a successful business but you're not sure how to get to the next level, I'm here to tell you that you're closer than you think. If you have a successful enterprise under your management of revenues with $10 million or below (by definition, a Main Street business), forget about looking for a place to start. You're already on the road; we're just going to give you a map.

••••

You might be surprised to hear that a large number of business owners whom I have worked with say the problem is, simply put, that no one ever told them what they needed to do; no one ever shared with them the roadmap. In response, I put together the **10 Steps for Joining The 2% Club.** With the Five Rules to guide you, and the 10 Steps in front of you, I believe that anyone with determination can join The 2% Club. I am not suggesting that joining The 2% Club will be easy—if it were, everyone would do it—but successful people do what unsuccessful people won't.

One metaphor that really works for me, in this regard, is running a marathon. Whether or not you're a couch potato or a weekend warrior, we all can envision marathon runners in our minds. Lean, disciplined, highly-trained and highly-motivated, they are the kind of uber-mensch that business owners—from Wall Street to Main Street—strive to be. But when you think of the work that they put into their craft, and the fact that the top marathon runners are professionals who do little else but work towards that goal, it's easy to think that it would be impossible for anyone but the most disciplined runner to complete the task successfully.

But the reality is, there is so much to be said for getting to that starting point and taking part in the race. It's true, not everyone is going to get their personal bests, and of those who do, those personal bests might be twice the time that it takes for the latest phenom from Kenya to complete the race. But what if you hadn't stepped up to the tape at all? The truth is that if you run the marathon—all 26.2 miles, at whatever your pace might be—you win. If you don't, you lose. The same can be said of walking the 10-step roadmap and following the five rules contained in this book, gleaned after years of research and pages upon pages of input from real-life success stories. The roadmap, together with the five rules, are the formula that creates your result; when followed, they become your custom definition of what you must accomplish to achieve your vision for success.

But, like the varied results of the marathon runners—both the tortoises and the hares—it's important to know that success is a wildly variable term, and it's not going to be the same for everyone. I say this not to let myself off the hook—I take my claims and my responsibility to you seriously—but for you to let yourself off the hook a little. You have to understand something about this approach, because it *is* a marathon, it's not a sprint: your vision of success has to be defined by you. You have to set the goals, and we can help you make them happen. Your success needs to be *your own* success. This is one of the secrets of The 2% Club that not everyone understands—the realization that the paths to success are there, waiting to be illuminated by our five rules, but that the paths are all varied and must be walked by their individual business owners. I can't run the race for you, but I can show you how to get to the finish line. Deciding to run the race is the first step, knowing that there isn't a cookie-cutter, one-size-fits-all approach for how you execute your strategy within these rules. The difference between the successful people and the unsuccessful people is simply that the unsuccessful people don't run the race. The 2% Club is gathered at the finish line, waiting for you to join them, no matter how long it takes you.

You just have to put one foot in front of the other.

••••

Before we show you the 10 Steps and delve into the Five Rules, we should talk a little bit more about what motivates the people in The 2% Club.

By nature, The 2% Club is made up of leaders, not followers. They are entrepreneurial in spirit, always looking for ways to make their businesses—and our world—better. Like the many paths to "winning" the marathon, the paths that they take to do this are varied and often winding, always conforming to what they need to achieve their success, rather than what might work for their neighbor.

What a lot of people might not realize about these 2%-ers,

particularly because they are all financially successful, is that while money is obviously the measuring stick that we have to resort to using for much of how we view success in business, the dollar signs are not the be-all, end-all. Entrepreneurs are motivated by success more than they are by fear of failure. An employee, or someone relatively low on the cubicle chain with no desire to manage, would be an example of someone who is motivated by fear of failure or loss of job. There's nothing wrong with that mode of work, but that isn't the mode that The 2% Club is operating in. These 2% want to lead. They want to succeed. And for them, that success isn't just about money.

For The 2% Club, success is about self-actualization, about being able to use their assets and investments to achieve their full potential—which includes their business—and the personal goals that are most important to them. If The 2% Club were to just look at money as the sole and major reporting metric with which they measured their success, they would most certainly make the fatal error of the remaining 98% and pour all of their money back into their business, hoping to achieve greater success down the line, without end.

You wouldn't be in the minority if you were to put this book down for a second and say to your nearest houseplant, "What's wrong with that? You need to spend money to make money!"

The answer comes from the aforementioned research into The 2% Club and the members' common traits. A major commonality is that these 2% of highly successful business owners see their business as the engine that drives their personal wealth; and rather than pouring all their money back into their business, they have a habit of developing, on average, 80% of their wealth *outside* their business. That might not make sense to the 98%, who are pouring all their money back into their business in hopes that somehow it will come back to them one day. By now, you should know what I have to say about that—that's why they're in the 98%.

The reason why The 2% Club has made so much effort into diversifying their assets, particularly where their business is concerned, is that even though the business itself may be successful, there's not a guarantee in the world that can save you from those dreaded "D-word" disasters. By developing their wealth outside of their businesses, these 2%-ers are self-actualizing. They are giving themselves the ability to control not only their businesses in the moment, but their lives in the future, and their decisions for the days and years to come.

While someone who has sunken all of his or her funds back into his or her business may be trapped in it until the day he or she dies, the members of The 2% Club don't have to. They can come and go on their own terms. They can pick their retirement date, choose who they want to sell the business to, and choose what kind of legacy they leave for their employees, their family, and themselves. Unlike those who have diversified, on the other hand, those who sink all of their assets back into their business might be lulled into a false sense of security. They feel like they are sitting on a big pot of gold that they can dump out at a moment's notice, but the truth is, and my research has shown, rainbows aren't the only thing that can disappear out of thin air—the pot of gold is sometimes the next thing to go, too. It's a well-known fact that the largest companies in the United States lost more than half of their value in just a six-month span from September 2008 to March 2009. For a very small business, that pot of gold can disappear even more quickly. I have personally witnessed many small businesses lose (or gain) even greater value in an even shorter period of time.

Consider this: Retirement portfolios are diversified. It's the nature of the beast. A good financial advisor won't let his or her client be exposed to too much risk by buying too much of any one thing. Likewise, a good business advisor wouldn't give the advice to a client that he or she should put all of his or her eggs in his or her business's basket. What happens if that business takes a turn for the worst? What happens if the value doesn't improve to what the client was expecting? What happens if a sudden medical issue prevents him or her from continuing at work and is forced to quick-sell the business?

Consider Frank, a conservative investor who has done his homework on his portfolio and has worked with his advisor to achieve diversity and risk management in his portfolio. He also owns a small chain of dry cleaning operations, all of which are running solidly in the black. While he has received advice from friends and relatives to expand his operations ("Why not? They're profitable! Are you crazy? As the economy gets better, things will only get better!" and so on and so on in a chorus of bullishness), he has resisted the temptation to sell off some of his retirement funds and use them to pour into expanding his business. He's nearing retirement age, after all, and he wants to be able to sell his business for what it's worth, and not accept some buyer's market lowball out of desperation. He holds steady, and diversifies his investments away from his business. He's able to retire when he's young and healthy enough to enjoy himself, taking his wife on the Caribbean cavorts she's always dreamed of having now that their children are all grown and provided for.

But what if Frank had listened to the devils on his shoulder? What if he had sauntered up to life's table and bet the farm, gone all in, pushed in all the chips and let them fall where they may?

It would be irresponsible to say that we know 100% for a fact that Frank would have failed, that he would have been unable to retire in the fashion he wanted to, that he would have been unable to provide for his wife the way he wanted to, that he would have been unable to come up on the right side of the dips and drops of a fickle marketplace. But since we're talking about percentages here, let's look at what we've found to be true through our years and years of research—the number of business owners who are able to achieve these goals are small. Remember the shrinking percentages?

Even if everything played out as well as could be for Frank as he decided to expand his business, there are some things that he couldn't possibly account for. What if Frank gets sick, or what if his wife gets sick? What if a new technology suddenly emerges in the market that makes it difficult for Frank's business to be profitable? What if changing tax structures and competition from cut-rate businesses reduce profitability in Frank's industry? If Frank's profitability declines by half, so would the value of his business. If he has poured all of his investments and assets into his business, that means that he's not just losing half of his invested money, he's losing half of the kingdom that he's worked so hard to build.

Not only does that put Frank a far cry from retiring comfortably, his self-actualization—and self-worth—is at an all-time low.

One of my major motivations for transforming my business into one that gives the advice of "The Missing Advisor" is that in over twenty years of managing my CPA firm, I've had the misfortune of watching these same, sad stories play out time and time again. I have witnessed many distressed business owners become disappointed, financially destroyed, and have their families torn apart as a result of the trap they've set for themselves. The story is usually the same—an overly confident entrepreneur, fired up about a new opportunity, blinded to the risks by the excitement of making it big, going all-in, and not being serious about following the Five Rules until it's too late. The ending is usually not very pretty. Many are left with no money and no options. The financial devastation takes an incredible toll on their families.

My work in helping people join The 2% Club has given me faith, and truly shown me that the doors to The 2% Club remain open to anyone willing to follow the Five Rules and put the 10 Steps into practice.

••••

What you'll find in these pages is different from the advice that you've gotten from your CPA or your investment advisor. While either one of those professionals' advice was valuable to you while you were building your business—the CPA's setting up a tax strategy that would help you maximize your bottom line and keep as much of your hard-earned money as you can and the investment planner's advising you on your portfolio—you're at the point where you need to take things one step further.

You may be pleased with what your current advisors are doing for you, but you probably feel like something is missing, like you are not getting certain advice that you need. If so, the information in the pages of this book could be what you are searching for. My firm's practices combine the expertise of the CPA with that of the financial advisor, while mixing in valuation and succession planning to produce something more forward-thinking and focused, something that Main Street business owners really need in order to break into the ranks of the 2%.

Included in this book, you'll find the roadmap—the 10 Steps to the promised land of the 2%, whether or not you're a big fish or a small fry. The advice that we give in these pages has been honed from years of advising businesspeople from all walks of life, but who have one very important thing in common: success on purpose.

Let your success be built on their experience.
Let your hard work open up all the doors that it's meant to.
Let yourself into the club.

CHAPTER 3

The Roadmap —
10 Steps for Joining The 2% Club

At the end of each chapter, I'll be giving you a little bit of homework. What I hope you get out of each of these exercises is a better sense of where you are on *your* journey to The 2% Club—and what you might still need to tackle in order to get you where you want to be. Each exercise is designed to help you cement each of the building blocks that we've gone over in the preceding chapter.

For this first chapter, the exercise is more of an introductory vessel for a concept that we'll be looking at throughout the book. The roadmap for joining The 2% Club is made up of ten steps—concrete action items that you can use to help you reach your ultimate goal. We've talked about the fact that The 2% Club follows five common rules, and we'll delve further into those rules as we go along.

As I've said before, the vision of The 2% Club isn't going to be the same for everyone, as such, the rules don't ensure the exact same result (only insofar as they insure success, whatever form that might take for you!). This is not a one-size-fits-all approach. These exercises will help you mold the path so that it fits your needs and goals.

What follows is a list of the steps and the rules you'll need to follow in order to get to The 2% Club. I want you to look at this simple list, taking time to evaluate where you are. If you feel like you're just starting out, that's okay. If you, like many of my clients, can tick off the first few steps and are looking for the final push, that's great, too.

The 2% Club Roadmap
Success on Purpose

Step #1	Establish Successful Business
Step #2	Achieve Personal Budget < 70% Income
Step #3	Establish Brokerage Account
Step #4	Purchase Commercial RE for Business
Step #5	Pay off Your Personal Residence
Step #6	Achieve Personal Budget < 50% Income
Step #7	Develop 80% of Wealth Outside Business
Step #8	Achieve Personal Budget < 3-5% Net Worth
Step #9	Sell, Transfer or Keep Your Business
Step #10	Welcome to The 2% Club!

Where do you fall on this continuum? What percentage of your income do you live on? What percent of your income do you invest? What steps have you completed? What's your timeline to take your next steps?

CHAPTER 4

The Five Rules of The 2% Club

Before you can complete the 10 Steps for Joining The 2% Club, you've got to learn the Five Rules. What we call "rules" are guidelines for keeping yourself—and your personal wealth—on the right track at each step along the way. This book is organized first and foremost around learning the Five Rules of The 2% Club. Once you learn the rules, following the 10 Steps becomes easier. In the final chapter of this book, we'll come back to the 10 Steps and give you some practical tips for creating your own plan for joining The 2% Club.

To get started, let's consider the five rules and more closely examine each of them.

RULE ONE: **Understand Business Valuation**

RULE TWO: **Use Tax Strategies That Build Wealth**

RULE THREE: **Develop Investments Outside Your Business**

RULE FOUR: **Stay Informed About Exit & Succession Planning**

RULE FIVE: **Protect Your Assets**

Understand Business Valuation

While the first rule of The 2% Club might seem like a no-brainer, I can assure you that, for whatever reason, the overwhelming majority of business owners (that's right: that 98% again!) never *really* get it. In order for your strategy to work, you must build a strong foundation, Step One. And while the first *step* in the process is to build a successful business, the first *rule* that will help cement that foundation is to truly know the value of your business. Without understanding and implementing the spirit of this rule, nothing that follows will really stick.

Now, what do we mean by *true value*? Am I trying to say that monetary markers aren't enough to calculate the value of the business you've built? Not exactly, but I am saying it's different than you might think. Time and time again, I've seen business owners make a crucial mistake when it comes to knowing the value of their business, and for those 98%, it has definitely come back to haunt them.

Believe it or not, there's one commonly perpetuated myth that eats away at this foundation, and that is that in business, bigger is always better. Business owners who have found a taste of success will often emphasize growth over all else in their plans and in their conception of their own value—expanding in size, locations, and employees, and using this sheer size as their primary benchmark for success. This is a mistake.

In business valuation, it's all about the cash flow. The cash flow is the major value driver by which accurate business valuations are determined. When a buyer is looking at your business, or you're shopping it around to prospects, they're all going to look for the same, largely tangible thing: What is the transferrable cash flow of your business? In even simpler terms, they want to know what's in it for them if they were to walk in tomorrow and take over. How much of their investment will come back to them each year after buying your business?

About 94% of businesses have less than $10 million in gross revenues, and 90% have less than $3 million in gross revenues. The average cash flow profit of a company with less than $3 million of sales is $150,000 (after paying the owner a fair market wage for his or her efforts), and those businesses sell for between three and five times their annual cash flow profit. That means that such a business could reasonably ask a buyer for between $450,000 to $750,000. Note again that this is not based on how many locations this business has, nor how many employees, nor how much the current owner *feels* that it might be worth in terms of *what they've put into it*. Ultimately, your business is worth the value of its future cash flows that can be transferred to the buyer. This is the buyer's return on the investment of purchasing your business. Even if you think your business is worth ten times as much as your valuation says it is worth, that doesn't mean it truly is. The cold, hard truth is that this game is all about value, and the quantifiable proof of that value is the cash flow.

Small business owners are notorious for thinking of their business as a "pot of gold," meaning that at the end of their rainbow, when they're ready to sail into their retirement years, they are planning on relying on their business sale to pay them back in spades. These owners are normally spending everything their business earns, living a high lifestyle and showing off their success, at the unfortunate expense of developing responsibly managed investments outside of the business. With blinders on and the gold shining brightly in their eyes, they think that the valuation of the business *must be* whatever they're going to need to retire on.

In reality, small businesses are not a wise investment vehicle to count on for your only retirement asset, just as you wouldn't think of exposing yourself to risk of loss by owning only one publicly traded stock. When you, as a business owner, focus solely on the value of your business as the means to provide for your retirement, you're probably going to wind up shooting yourself in the foot.

A lot of business owners come to me when they're ready to retire at sixty-five or seventy years old, and they think that their business is going to be their golden ticket. "Here you go," they say to me, sliding their own valuation figures across the table.

I can't begin to tell you how tired I got of seeing their faces fall when I explained to them that their business was only "worth" about three to five years of cash flow, and that, if they don't have any other investments, the business sale will only pay for about three to five years of their lifestyle in retirement. Whereas other owners (and members of The 2% Club) come to me with real estate and a diversified stock portfolio along with their business, the overwhelming 98% are spending everything their business makes, effectively putting all their eggs in just that one basket.

Take one example: we had a client, we'll call him Todd, who was doing about $9 million a year in sales with his small business when we engaged him. After paying for all his expenses, he was left earning about $500,000 a year net, which made his business worth about $2 million at the point that we started working together. When I sat him down to ask what his goals were, he had them in his mind as clear as day: He wanted to increase his revenue by substantial numbers and his strategy to do it was to be a cost leader, to undercut the competition by selling his products for a lower price. To that end, he said, he was opening up a second location, doubling his number of employees and requiring a new layer of management that didn't currently exist. He was successful in achieving his goal and increased revenues from about $9 million to $20 million.

At the same time that Todd was increasing his revenues, he spent massive amounts of money, liquidating other investments and dumping the money into his business to pay for opening the second location. He increased payroll, overhead, added more management and increased other expenses to go along with lower prices. He spent a lot of money on advertising to attract a cost-sensitive customer in a new location that was totally unfamiliar to him. Consequently, he ended up reducing his profitability to about $100,000 a year. When he came back to us to show us his increased revenue, it nearly broke my heart to have to tell him the detrimental effects he had wrought on his business value. The strategy employed by business owners like Todd is focused on increased revenue and size of operations, rather than on profitability. To create value in your business (and wealth for yourself) you must create value for your customer first, and volume second. This value will make itself apparent by being able to charge higher prices and will result in a strong bottom line profit.Companies like Apple and Microsoft know that price is only an issue in the absence of value. They created great value for their customers first and large volume second, making them two of the most profitable companies in the world. Todd and his compatriots focused so rabidly on competing as a low-price leader that they ended up hacking their own bottom line to bits. Focusing on increasing volume, just from a cost-competition perspective—which is unfortunately a common strategy both in the marketplace and in the academic literature at this point—reduces the *value* of your business. A bit counter-intuitive, since the *volume* has gone up, but again, you'd be focusing on the wrong v-word, which is the situation we found Todd getting stuck in.

Todd listened to what I had to say and went to work attempting to reverse the course of his mistake. But unfortunately, by the time we had this discussion, the damage was done. Todd had built his business in his new location by attracting price-shopping, cost-driven consumers looking for the best buy on a homogeneous product, rather than loyal customers who were provided something uniquely valuable. He painted himself into a corner, unable to raise prices for fear of losing his customers and making matters worse. Todd poured his money into the company to create larger size, more revenues, and another location. The result was a company worth one-fifth the previous value and the loss of his money from the investments he had liquidated.

A strategy of competing on low price with a homogeneous product is a sure way to just attract cost-conscious clients that essentially run the value down right under your nose (and by your own invitation). And this is where rule number one—understanding business valuation—really comes into play.

With information comes knowledge, and with knowledge, power. If Todd had followed in the footsteps of The 2% Club from the beginning, he would have been proactive in his creation of value, steering his ship on a much better course rather than wrecking it on the sharp rocks of hubris that got him in the end. My work with The 2% Club has produced some quick tips that can help small business owners eventually reap the rewards of their hard work, if only they do a little preparation on the front end. Here, we'll assume that you have a viable, successful business and you're interested in preparing it for sale somewhere down the road. To do that, you'll need to heed these tips.

Tips for Increasing the Value of Your Business

1. Create value first, volume second
2. Cash flow profit is king
3. Tax returns matter
4. Start early
5. Focus on profitability
6. Think of value as a range
7. Make decisions that increase visible value

1. Create value first, volume second

As business owners, we've all heard of the big company that bought the little company for a huge price. This is a called a *strategic value sale*. Every business owner would love to sell his business for a strategic value, but the odds of doing so with a Main Street business (one with less than $10 million of annual sales) are about as good as winning the lottery. Strategic value sales are common for middle-market companies (ones with $10 to $500 million of annual sales), but are very rare on Main Street. Companies that compete based on low price are even less likely to get a strategic sale; it's simply too easy for the competition to replicate your business without having to buy it. To successfully accomplish a strategic sale, you increase your odds substantially if you focus on creating value for the customer first, and then allow yourself to be acquired by a business that can increase your volume substantially. In doing so, the acquiring business can create a huge return for themselves and are able to share that with you through the strategic sale price.

2. Cash flow profit is king

Almost all small businesses will sell for a *financial value* rather than a strategic value. A financial value is simple to calculate; it represents three to five years of transferable cash flow profit. The greater the transferable cash flow profit, the greater the financial value of the business. The cash flow profit represents the return on investment to the buyer, and the purchase of the business represents the investment. If the cash flow profit is 20% of the purchase price each year, then it takes five years to return the investment of the purchase price—a 20% rate of return. Purchasing a business for three years of cash flow is a 33% return on investment, meaning it will take three years to return the investment. Small businesses generally demand a 20-33% rate of return, and it is this return that drives the value. A smart business owner may hope for a strategic sale but will not bet the farm on it, instead opting to plan for a financial value sale.

3. Tax returns matter

To a buyer (and, let's not forget, the buyer's financer), your tax returns are going to be the most important source of information involved in the deal. The Main Street business world is littered with stories about businesses not closing their sale because the buyer shows up and the seller doesn't have a reliable tax return to show them—maybe just a scribble on a sheet of paper here and there. While this is an extreme example, to the buyer, there is no bigger red flag than a sloppy set of books and tax returns. Their defenses go up, they worry about the risk, and they feel that there's no evidence that there's going to be a good enough return on their investment. The chances of that sale happening are slim.

How your tax returns are prepared definitely matters. Different CPAs will always have different philosophies on how to correctly prepare your returns. But no matter what tack they take, it should go without saying that the figures need to be credible, verifiable, and accurate. You want your tax returns to show a trend (not just an outlier or high year every so often) of increasing positive net income. Businesses, in this regard, are like stocks—buyers like to grab them when they're going up and will be scared to buy them when they are going down. The buyer, the business valuator, and the bank that will most likely be providing a large portion of the cash in your sale, are looking for a continually improving value and a certain level of stability.

4. Start early

You got into business because you're a savvy person, because you can anticipate needs and what it takes to fulfill those needs. You should treat your work in understanding and molding the value of your business in precisely the same way that you'd treat an unmet need in the marketplace—by studying, understanding, anticipating, and *acting* on that information. In order to get the most work out of your tax returns, and in order to make sure you're going in the right direction to begin with, you're going to need to start this process early.

Laying the groundwork for establishing value in your business with your tax returns needs to begin several years before you ultimately plan to sell the business. The buyer, the bank, and the valuator will read your tax returns to learn the story they tell about your business. Setting performance goals in your business so that your tax returns tell the story you want them to in the future is an important part of planning your entry into The 2% Club.

Aside from cash flow and solid tax returns, there are several other benefits that could make your business easier to sell, but not necessarily make it more valuable. Ask yourself this: Would doing XYZ make the business *more* attractive to a buyer, or would it simply encumber your sales pitch down the line? If the answer is the former, then go for it. If you think it might be the latter, then you should sit down with your advisors and model how it might play out. Remember, though, in spite of all things you could do to make your business more attractive to a buyer, cash flow will likely be the limiting factor on your business's value.

In Todd's case, if he had understood that profit needed to be his central focus, he might have acted differently, positioning his business more on a value basis than volume. Being willing to lay the groundwork properly means really understanding the fact that if you don't build your business right the first time, you will have to tear it apart and start over. Once in a while, you'll come across a business that reinvents itself, but those success stories are few and far between; reinvention is an extremely painful process. When you spend the next twenty to thirty years of your life slowly building a business, you want it to be worth money when you're done. And those strategic decisions that you're making in the early stages are the foundation of that worth.

So just how big should your business be? The 2% Club shows us that the approach is to establish a business that is just the right size—not necessarily a *large* business, but a solid, healthy business just big enough to provide for your lifestyle and the accumulation of assets outside your business. To determine the right size for you, consider that the members of The 2% Club don't spend all their profits. They don't even spend anywhere *near* what those businesses make. Refer back to The 2% Club Roadmap. It shows that The 2% Club achieves a personal budget of less than 50% of their income. So to determine the right size of business, you should double your personal budget and use that as a profit goal.

For The 2% Club, it's not a matter of endless growth or luck; it's a matter of strategy and following the rules.

5. Focus on profitability

By now, you've seen that The 2% Club uses the profitability of their business to drive its value. If Todd had been able to double his profitability, rather than his size, he would have been able to double the business value.

Apart from increasing the value to a prospective buyer, when you are able to increase the profitability of your business, that means that you can also garner more profit to invest outside your business every year. These investments should be done as safely and wisely as possible. The investments should be diversified and used strategically, rather than just dumped back into the business to increase the size.

By doubling your profit, not only will you have a significant portion of your income available to invest, it should double the value of your business. The combined effect is a substantial increase to your wealth.

Now *that's* thinking like a 2%-er.

6. Think of value as a range

This tip is designed to create responsiveness to what can frequently be a moving target. In order to get the upper hand when it comes to riding off into the sunset after closing a great deal, you'll need to consider this tip early on in the process.

One of the things that I always tell my clients who come to me for their business valuation is that they should think of value as a range. This means identifying their most ideal buyer—a buyer who is able to buy the business at the high end of this range of value. For most small businesses, this means an insider, such as an employee or a co-owner. An ideal buyer has knowledge of your business, and as a result, has a great deal more confidence than an outsider or neophyte would. This confidence enables them to take the leap without as much aversion to the risk; because they're familiar with the lay of the land, the risk simply isn't there as much for them as it would be for an outsider.

Unlike strategic sales of middle market companies where

outsiders are the best buyers, on Main Street, outsiders fall at the lower end of your value range. They come in automatically more leery of the proposition of taking a chance on buying your business and are often looking to low-ball the price and steal it away. When dealing with an outsider, you're going to find a lot of tire kicking, looking under the hood, and even feet dragging before the deal closes. And could you blame them? This is a *major* decision, and even though you might get a little jumpy and feel insulted when they offer you a price that's at the low end of your value range, this is the reality of dealing with an outsider. They usually aren't your ideal buyer, but you do need to consider that they are *a* buyer, and if you can't find your ideal buyer, you will need to plan for the fact that your business might be going to sell at their level. This should shape your planning. If you notice that your fish might be biting at this end of the value range, then you're going to have to adjust your future financial plans accordingly. If you've been thinking like a member of The 2% Club, you're going to be better positioned to deal with a shortfall than someone who has been blindly marching forth thinking that the best case scenario is the only scenario for which they should prepare. There's a significant difference in net value between these two scenarios, and so it's important for you to think about, early on, how you can develop a market for your business—brainstorming and positioning it to highlight as many benefits as possible to attract your most ideal buyer.

7. Make decisions that increase visible value

This brings us to our last tip, which, like the others, can be seen as an action item for you to think about and put into practice.

Maybe you've just read the last tip and think that you're all set—that your business is ripe fruit for your ideal buyer. If that's the case, then my hat is off to you—keep doing what you're doing. If, however, you think there's a little room for improvement and you have been able to ferret this out far enough in advance of your proposed sale date, then you're probably wondering how you can turn the tide and position yourself a little more advantageously.

When clients come to me and say that they are getting ready to offer their business for sale, I typically gather up three years of business tax returns, from which I begin to prepare the business valuation that we provide, and while I'm doing that, I have them go off on their own to write a company overview. While I'm concerning myself with the monetary value, the client then sets to work trying to quantify some of the less obvious, though no less important, benefits.

It's crucial that this company overview be stocked full of exciting benefit statements for the buyer and portrays an exciting vision of the future of the company where the new owner can see himself at the helm. The business owners who really excel at this exercise almost always come back to me with a concrete, truly valuable list of items that the business has at *present*, alongside a clear-cut vision for the future. In their company overview (a benefits statement for buyers), these business owners are able to get their prospect really excited about where their business is going, and why the skies are looking blue for a good long time to come.

I've had less successful clients come back to me with resumes about how great they are. But here's the hard truth that I'm faced with telling them: your buyer doesn't care about how great you are, because you're going out the door. As crazy as it sounds, I rarely meet a buyer who doesn't think they can run the business better than the person who's running it now. Most sellers will disagree, but this is not their problem; it is the buyer's risk to take. Focus on benefit statements that get the buyer excited about *his or her own* prospects for the business, about the vision of *his or her* future. Following this tip means keeping your ideal buyer in mind as you make decisions on what benefits to install in your business, so that they are ones that appeal to your ideal buyer when the time comes to sell.

••••

One of the great things about working as a consultant in this capacity is that I've been able to see some of those success stories that have walked the path to The 2% Club. I have discovered that many entrepreneurs, when equipped with the knowledge of what truly creates value in their business, will find a way to create the value they want. One such story is about a pair of partners who, unlike Todd, had laid the groundwork early and had time on their side—they made the right moves, adjusted when they had to, and came out on the other side all the better for it.

Mark and Larry had a wonderful business that was doing well locally; they had sizable revenues and multiple product lines. They came to us for a valuation, and we saw their business as being worth a little under $500,000. Our conversations with them focused on what the value drivers of their business were: profitability, benefits like transferability of staff, the stability of the profit stream, and so on. We emphasized to them that their value had nothing to do with size and that they needed a solid rate of return if they were going to increase their value.

They took all of that knowledge, went back to their business, and did a lot of thinking about what made their business unique, valuable, and viable for the future. They decided that they had one primary core product that was very strong, whereas two other product lines were taking up a lot of their time and resources. Although they were proud of everything they offered, the effort for those other two product lines was really killing their bottom line. So they made the decision to abandon them, and focus on doing what they did best.

In doing so, they were able to substantially reduce their expenses and increase their sales per client, eventually tripling their profit and the value of their business over the next two years. Mark and Larry's business is worth about $1.5 million as of this writing, and the positive press in their field is only growing, too. It goes without saying that they've got buyers chomping at the bit to take on their business. This is one of my favorite success stories, as Mark and Larry were able to understand how their valuation was done, what it meant, what they could do to increase their business's value, and were able to substantially improve that value.

The key distinction between this story and Todd's story is that Mark and Larry's is focused on profitability, while Todd's was not. Mark and Larry focused on the product that had the greatest value to their customers, allowing them to improve profitability, thereby increasing the value of their business. Todd merely increased volume, and we've seen time and time again that bigger is not necessarily better. You must create customer value first, as evidenced by a strong price, and volume second. If you miss the first step, you wind up like Todd.

The bottom line? In order to establish a successful business and then eventually sell that business at a beneficial price, you have to understand the difference between those two stories. And once that foundation is laid, you've got a great start on a very promising future.

WORKSHEET:
Understanding Business Valuation

Think about the previous chapter as you answer these questions and assess yourself on the following points. If you feel you're positioned strongly, take that confidence and bank it as we roll into the future together. If you feel you need to do some repositioning, now may be the time to do that!

1. What value does your business create in the mind of its customers, making you different from competition, which allows you to charge higher prices?

2. By narrowing your focus, can you innovate ways to create more customer value, simplifying your business and making it more profitable?

3. Once you have simplified and created greater value and higher prices, can you multiply those results?

4. Have you recently had a business valuation? What were the results, and do you understand the critical factors that drive value for your business?

5. Have you been keeping accurate, up-to-date tax documentation for your business? Does this show an upward trend or a downward trend?

6. Who is your ideal buyer? What range would you hope to get in a sale?

7. What is valuable about your business to your ideal buyer?

8. Imagine yourself in the future and that you are preparing to sell your business, write the company overview "stocked full of benefits" statements for your buyers. This is your vision of the business you want to create.

RULE TWO:

Use Tax Strategies that Build Wealth

You've done the work and put in the time. Your foundation is strong—you've established a successful business as outlined in the first step of your roadmap to The 2% Club, and part of establishing that successful business has been creating a valuable proposition for your customers and your ideal buyer down the line. You may feel, now, nine steps yet to take, that you still have your work cut out for you—and you do!

However, it's important to take stock of what you've done. You've made it to a crucial juncture on the journey that most don't ever find, despite searching high and low. If you've come this far down the road, the rest won't necessarily be downhill, but with the foundation of a valuable (and properly valuated) business, you'll be in better shape to contend with the challenges that lie ahead.

The second rule that The 2% Club employs is all about building your wealth by minimizing one of the largest expenses of any successful investment—taxes. Like the first rule, this is something that these business winners are doing *proactively*, forecasting trends and looking ahead, rather than struggling to catch up once they've already fallen behind. By using tax strategies that build wealth, The 2% Club is able to ensure not only that their business and personal financial houses stay strong in the present, but also a brighter, more sustainable future by capitalizing on the luxuries of time and interest.

Rule Two will greatly accelerate your success on the next three steps on our roadmap to joining The 2% Club:

- **Step Two:** achieving a personal budget that's less than 70% of your income;

- **Step Three:** establishing a brokerage account; and

- **Step Four:** purchasing commercial real estate for your business.

By moving through these steps—one at a time, building slowly and solidly upon each step—you will emerge with a solid base for your tax benefit strategy, one that will keep pushing you along on your quest for success and a place in The 2% Club.

••••

Most people don't realize that, according to the 2010 census, the 90th percentile of household income is $135,000 per year. The same data tells us that the 75th percentile of household income in this country is $80,000 per year. I'm not sure why this comes as a surprise to so many people, but if the economic bubble that burst in 2008 was any indication, I'm willing to bet it has to do with our overwhelming desire for *more*—more possessions, more money, more space, more everything. I think that when many people in the upper echelons of income hear those numbers, it's hard for them to process, because they're making upwards of $300,000 per year and still feel like they're poor, not realizing that they're well above the average household income. It could indeed be that $300,000 isn't enough for them to feel like they're living well, but if you look at the averages, at that point, I think you'd have to assume that the income isn't the problem, the expenses are.

As I noted earlier, the instinct to move away from the mountains of more is part of what sets The 2% Club apart. They want to work smarter, not harder; and they know the difference between volume and value. *They* aren't surprised, then, when I tell them that the average income of 90% of all businesses in the United States is around $150,000 per year—and that a 2% Club business owner with that average income invests nearly 50% of their total household income and still lives a better lifestyle than 75% of the households in our country. This isn't news to them—*they're doing this already.*

Before you can truly move on to worrying about tax strategies and further investments, you need to make sure that you're living as The 2% Club does: making wise decisions, trimming the fat both on your personal *and* business budget, and not giving in to the siren song that so many fall victim to when their wallets start getting a little fatter. Having a lean budget and a lean lifestyle doesn't mean going without, it simply means that you're going to have less of a shortfall to make up for if anything should happen to you, your family, or your business; second, assuming you have a long and successful career, you're going to have all that more to invest and enjoy on the back end.

Now, some readers may ask why I'm asking them to achieve a *personal* budget of less than 70% of their total household income. The reason is simple: in order to accumulate wealth, you must have income to invest. The 2% Club lives quite modestly so that they can invest. My research has shown that what you get at work, you get at home, and vice versa. Business owners tend to run their households with the same energy and philosophy that they do their businesses. The 2% Club is full of examples of this kind of behavior—you're not going to find a successful businessman in The 2% Club who can't run his household like the same tight business ship. Chaos and disorder in one bleeds into the other, especially when you get to a point where you might be running up against some of those unforeseen emergencies either in your personal life or your business life. The reality of The 2% Club is that smart spending and an aversion to debt is habitual, and that goes for the home front as well as the headquarters.

As a result of achieving Step Two, you'll see a stronger balance sheet. You can start seeing the benefits of your frugal (but not spendthrift) decisions to focus on your value drivers while cutting out the excess. You'll see your cash reserves growing, good numbers on the receivable side, dwindling or no numbers on the payable side, and very little to no long-term debt. With this solid positioning, you'll be able to start investing the other 30% of your income. Initially, much of that 30% may go back into your business, and as long as those decisions are truly value-driven or focused on paying off debt to strengthen the business's balance sheet and bottom line, that's fine. But remember, The 2% Club carries investments *outside* of the business, creating a healthy, balanced portfolio.

Once this step has been completed, you will be financially fit enough to benefit from tax strategies that build your wealth. In this chapter, I've gathered some examples—in the form of tips—of such advantageous strategies for you, although there are certainly more nuanced issues that can be parsed out with your advisor down the line.

Tips for Reducing Taxes to Help Build Your Wealth

1. Explore options for compensation planning
2. Explore options for converting to cash basis
3. Establish a non-tax-deferred investment account
4. Tax loss harvesting is a down market opportunity
5. Purchase commercial real estate for your business

1. Explore options for compensation planning

Compensation planning is the first, and perhaps most impor-tant, tax strategy that builds wealth. Proper compensation planning can create a benefit stream that never ends. If you're employing a strategy that saves money every year on taxes, that money can then be invested, accumulating wealth.

Let's look at the example of John, a forty-year-old self-employed consultant who makes $80,000 per year. He came to my firm to complete a tax review with one of our advisors, during which we determined that if he converted to an S-Corporation and paid himself a reasonable wage, he could potentially save up to $5,000 per year on taxes.

Taking a longer-term view of things, he looked at the path he hoped to take over the next twenty years. John knew that he wanted to work at least another twenty years, and so the investment returns that would be possible on a $5,000 per year chunk of change were considerable. Assuming that John was able to invest the full $5,000 each year—something that he should be able to do if he's keeping his operating budget and personal expenses lean and clean—a modest 8% return on those investments would bring the end value of his investments-via-savings to over $250,000. That is no small accomplishment. In just a short consultation, John was able to improve his projected retirement wealth by a quarter of a million dollars—a source of wealth that would have gone untapped were he to leave the S-corp option on the table.

It's best to make use of this tip and the one that follows after you've completed a reliable business valuation with the records to back it up as noted in Rule One. Those records are what you're going to need in order to prove to the IRS that your compensation analysis, and therefore your compensation, is a fair and reasonable one.

2. Explore options for converting to cash basis

Another tax strategy to consider employing now for a brighter future is converting your accounting from accrual to cash basis for the purposes of your tax return reporting. Exercising this option can allow you to achieve a significant one-time tax savings.

Consider the example of Henry, a business owner who, for more than twenty years, has owned and operated a construction related business. Henry has spent the past two decades employing the strategies of his fellow 2% Club members—making sure to always look forward, rather than leaving himself in a vulnerable position to scramble to make up lost time and cash when it's plainly too late. Henry has built a successful business with an eye on creating value for his eventual buyer.

It so happens that Henry has been fortunate enough to snag the ideal buyer that I talked about in the last chapter. His construction manager has been planning to buy the business. Henry, like others, came to us to obtain a business valuation for the purpose of determining a fair price to ask. While preparing his valuation we reviewed his tax positions and determined that Henry was able to recognize a significant one-time tax savings of $225,000, and this benefit could be created before the sale went through: A change in tax laws now allows most businesses with less than $10 million in gross annual revenue, to convert their accounting systems from an accrual to a cash basis. Had this been missed, Henry would have left that money on the table for his *buyer* to enjoy after the sale.

Other tax strategies can be put in place when executing a sale, all of which should point towards generating the highest net proceeds (money in your pocket after taxes) as possible. Your advisor should be able to help you navigate these waters, but the important thing to remember is that if you haven't built a strong foundation with a successful business and kept an eye on your long-term planning, these options may not be available to you when the time comes to cash in.

3. Establish a non-tax-deferred investment account

Many people have an unfortunate view of investing that fails to account for all of the options. Like those who are blind to certain advantageous tax strategies, it's not uncommon to find otherwise savvy businesspeople who think that the only option for investing is socking the maximum tax-deferred amount into an IRA or 401k for each year. Smart business owners round out their portfolios with brokerage accounts. These accounts allow you to invest in the market with non-tax-deferred money, which, unlike tax-deferred accounts, is liquid and can be cashed out without penalty. This liquidity provides you with the cash you will need to seize opportunities when they come up, buying assets for less in down markets. With a brokerage account, you can simultaneously reduce your tax bill through tax-loss harvesting while building long-term wealth, something that you'll be able to do more of if you're actively decreasing your expenses and investing more of those savings outside of your business. The next two tips offer strategies for converting these brokerage assets into tax savings that helps build your wealth.

4. Tax loss harvesting is a down market opportunity

Consider Mark, a successful land surveyor who started his business fifteen years ago. When he began his business, he quickly stepped into the mindset of a 2% Club member, slowly investing in high-quality funds through a taxable brokerage account in addition to his tax-deferred savings. Ten years ago, when he came into some land as payment for a work project, he was able to add that to his portfolio. Now his portfolio contains a mix of stocks, real estate, and income from his business—and he's keeping a good balance, not leaning too heavily on any one of those segments.

In 2008, when the market crashed and Mark's funds plunged to nearly 50% value, he was understandably discouraged. He had made the investment in these funds thinking long-term, but was as fearful as anyone would be when there are big declines in stock market investments. He wasn't trying to time the market or game the system; he's just a hardworking guy who knew a market-diversified portfolio was a good way to invest.

Mark's advisor kept him focused on the future, taking a long-term view like the one that Mark had displayed when he purchased the funds in the first place. He reminded Mark that dramatic stock market declines have historically been followed by dramatic rebounds—it's the cycle of the entire market, he reminded Mark. Since Mark was invested in funds that collectively represented the entire market, the entire financial system would have to fail in order for him to lose his investment, and it's a good long-term bet that the financial system won't fail.

Mark was fearful, but agreed to retain his exposure, thankfully, and when the stock market began to rise not even a year later, he still enjoyed the benefits of his investments gaining in value. But one of the key things that Mark and his advisor were able to do was harvest some of the paper losses that Mark took when his investment funds plunged by selling them off and replacing them with funds that had similar market exposure, but were different. These paper-only capital losses carry forward indefinitely and can be used against future gains; it's like banking tax deductions for the future. This way, Mark was able to harvest significant tax write-offs from some of those stock losses, and he could capitalize on those write-offs when it came time to sell the land plots that he owned, or his business, thus avoiding most of the capital gains taxes associated with those sales.

It is rare to see Main Street investment and tax professionals working together closely enough to successfully execute this tactic. It's a tax strategy that seems to fall through the cracks that exist between the domains of these two advisors.

5. Purchase commercial real estate for your business

At first blush, this may seem contrary to the advice and strategies you've read about so far. But in no way am I advocating needlessly expanding your volume; as we saw in the previous chapter, that's not a wise decision for your bottom line and it *definitely* isn't something that you'd catch The 2% Club doing. Also, like everything else, there are caveats to consider when taking a step forward to ensure you're taking the *right* step forward.

Let's consider Jennifer, whose successful restaurant has been open for business for three years. When we met, Jennifer was leasing her space, but was eyeing a commercial property to purchase where she could operate her restaurant, thus becoming totally self-sufficient as a business owner with no landlord to answer to.

When a storefront a few doors down from Jennifer's current location went on the market, she jumped on the chance to buy it. The sale price of the property was $400,000, and in order to get the best financing possible, the bank she was using for her loan required her to make a down payment of 35%. Jennifer had a strong cash position going into the deal as a result of having been successful at Steps One, Two, and Three on the roadmap, and she could have made more than the required down payment. The new location came with significant fixtures, signage & kitchen equipment. By allocating a significant portion of the $400,000 purchase cost to these items she was able to realize significant short-term tax write-offs, creating significant cash tax refunds that could be returned to her investment accounts while obtaining a real estate asset that would increase in value.

Like the other stories I've mentioned in this chapter, you'll see that Jennifer is playing it smart, looking long-term, and trying to maximize the amount of income that she can make and keep (and thus, save and eventually invest) by using tax strategies appropriate to her situation. Because of those tax write-offs, when spread out over the following five-year period, Jennifer was able to pay significantly less income tax on the income generated by her restaurant. At the end of those five years, when the building she now owned was appraised for $1 million, she decided to sell the *business* to a new owner and lease out the real estate. Jennifer now has an asset that will continue to appreciate over time (for the most part, crash of 2008 caused by rampant speculation aside, real estate *does* appreciate). This asset is an attractive income stream that makes sense—it wasn't a stretch, it wasn't a choice of expansion, and it will continue to pump up her portfolio over time. That same portfolio, by the way, is now diversified away from the original source—her restaurant business—and now includes real estate as well as her brokerage account. Now, like the rest of The 2% Club, she's free to look at other opportunities, and the future is bright.

WORKSHEET:
Use Tax Strategies That Build Your Wealth

1. Think of your personal budget. Is it 70% of your income? Less, more?

2. If it's more than 70% of your income and you're at the beginning of your process, can you increase income without increasing your budget, or are their some things you can cut or re-position to save money?

3. Are you employing all available tax strategies to minimize your tax burden?

4. Are you reviewing your tax strategies during the year with your advisor and making adjustments?

5. Are you diversified financially—do you have liquidity by investing in a brokerage account?

6. Do you understand the significant tax benefits of business owner occupied real estate?

Develop Investments Outside Your Business

One of the reasons that entrepreneurs are so successful at what they do is that they have that kernel of strength inside them that allows them to take risks. This is not the same thing as the wealth of experience and knowledge that they amass over their lifetime as a successful businessperson. Rather, an entrepreneur dreams big, and knows that to accomplish those big dreams, he or she needs to be able to take risks to achieve them. Some individuals are more conservative about everything—from their investments to the risks they take in their own business. Some people are employees—content to answer to someone else and let *that* person take the risks if the business should falter. There is absolutely nothing wrong with these people. They have their own philosophy and their own values. However, these are not the qualities that make up an entrepreneur.

By now, you should know that I'm not saying that entrepreneurs should take *every* risk. Far from it. The membership rolls of The 2% Club are full of people who have taken intelligent, measured risks and have hedged their bets appropriately. Their risks have been rewarded. And part of the reason for this reward is that they took risks not as a lottery player takes risks, but as a smart businessperson takes risks.

As an entrepreneur, you need to be keenly aware of your appetite for risk. Most entrepreneurs, at some point, have considered all of their assets up for grabs when it comes to risk-taking and investment in the business. Even members of The 2% Club are not immune and are frequently tempted to offer a large cash infusion into a new business venture. But unlike many bullish entrepreneurs in the 98% who would bet the farm, The 2% Club seem to recognize that they have enough risk owning a small business and rarely pony up more than a third of their wealth for new business ventures.

Another all-too-common statistic that gets bandied around is the rate of divorce caused by disputes revolving around money. The number one reason for divorce, in fact, is differences regarding money. While some entrepreneurs, like those bullish business owners I mentioned above, think that all of their assets should be liquidated and poured into the business—or put up for collateral for business loans—their spouses often occupy a spot at the other side of the spectrum, and are more apt to be conservative, security-minded people. The 2% Club entrepreneurs sense that their portfolio already includes a risky small business and they mitigate this risk by investing outside their business. In doing so, they establish financial security for their spouse, their family, their employees and themselves. I believe their marriages are stronger as a result of having less exposure to disputes revolving around money. They know that they have a responsibility to be financially secure for those who depend on them, and that's not going to change just because times might be good for a while. In fact, 2% Club members are always thinking ahead, navigating those dreaded "what ifs"—and they know that if times get tough, the pressure to provide is only going to increase.

By executing the following steps on the roadmap to The 2% Club—paying off your personal residence (Step Five), achieving a personal budget of less than 50% of your income (Step Six), and developing 80% of your wealth *outside* of your business (Step Seven)—you are following the third rule: Develop Investments Outside of Your Business. By following this rule, you're not only well on your way to ensuring the viability of your business, but also protecting some of your most precious assets: the people who depend upon you for their safety and financial security.

••••

As I've mentioned, Step Five on the roadmap is the first step to conquer for this chapter. By paying off your house, you then develop wealth outside of your business and establish financial security all in one blow. While I concede that the recent market crash and subsequent recession resulting from the hyper-speculation of the real estate market has lead to dire consequences, for the most part, real estate is a good investment. I don't mean that you should consider your home equity to be your retirement portfolio, but what I do mean is that it's always a good idea to pay down your debts and keep your monthly operating budget—as a household, as in your business—as low as possible. Paying off your mortgage helps you achieve this. Two-percenters generally don't buy ostentatious homes with more space and features than they need, either, so when they are paying off their mortgage, they're paying off a reasonable, conservative investment that should be in line with their means.

The benefits of paying off your mortgage don't stop there, however; it becomes a good sort of snowball, a self-fulfilling prophecy of momentum and debt reduction, allowing you to reduce your monthly expenses after the payments have been made. This will help you live on less than 50% of your income, the very crucial sixth step on the path to The 2% Club. Typically, an active home mortgage will represent a monthly outcome that costs most people 25-45% of their household income—a significant portion. Free from the burden of a monthly house payment, you will be able to accumulate wealth, investing more of it in the appropriate channels and giving you extraordinary leverage. With time and the power of compounding returns on your side, the positive cash flow you are creating will help your balance sheet increase like gangbusters. None of this would be possible if you were still putting that extra cash towards your mortgage payment—or other reoccurring expenses like car payments or credit card balances. Investing in your home is money well spent—not excessive cash flung in the face of a depreciating purchase.

Around the time that a 2%-er is able to pay off his mortgage, he is usually five to ten years into ownership of commercial real estate, as I've advocated in earlier chapters. Owning that commercial real estate is another excellent notch in his belt, a vital part of a well-rounded portfolio. Having his hands in the commercial real estate as well as the personal real estate pots, and having considerable equity in both, then, is a diversified position that will pay off in the end. It's important to remember that when the housing market is down, it doesn't necessarily mean the business real estate market will be down—and by owning his own space, he is saving on costs and building equity there, too. This good equity position means a certain level of comfort, and again, certain savings that can be added to his investment larder.

At this point, the business has already proven to be successful—a cash-generating machine. The person at its helm (and again, feel free to imagine yourself here—this visualization won't be at all off the mark if you can self-actualize and accomplish the steps and strategies in this book) is making smart decisions, saving cash, and streamlining expenses. Their business and their personal and professional real estate holdings have taken up valuable time—time that they've spent building a strong foundation and an advantageous position. Standing from this strong foundation, they are now able to tackle the next step, Step Seven: Develop 80% of your wealth outside of your business.

If you're here, or nearly here, on the roadmap, this is where it's especially important that you receive some sound advice on how to allocate those assets that you've spent all this time building up. I've found that at this point on the journey, most business owners will turn to the stock market, regardless of how much or how little risk tolerance they have. They don't turn to the stock market because they love it, they recognize it as a necessary evil to protect, preserve, and grow their wealth. They avoid advisors who love the stock market and select advisors who understand that speculation and market timing are sure ways to erode performance. They choose advisors who stick to the fundamentals of simplicity, good diversification, low fees and proper asset allocation. Overly aggressive asset allocation strategies may take dramatic turns when an investor can least afford the fluctuation, as in the case that one's family emergency might coincide with a downward spiral in the market. Overly conservative asset allocation strategies, on the other hand, may not perform well enough to provide for the investor and his family in the long run, when his health or his plans take him away from the day-to-day pressures of running the business.

At this juncture, these business owners will park new cash in the stock market. They've assessed the other options—opening another business, gaining more real estate—and correctly judged that the former option is heavily-laden with risk and more work, and the latter is illiquid and takes away more of their valuable time than the stock market will. It seems the business owner, and the money, are at an impasse.

So what's a hard working person to do to make sure that their investments are working hard as well? As I've said before, there's no one-size-fits-all approach to gaining this success, but I do know that by following the following tips culled from years of researching The 2% Club, there is a smart approach. This approach can be tailored to your business, your specific situation, your dreams, your plans, and your life. The market is a necessary evil—one that you must face armed with all the information, a level head, and an appropriate advisor or advisor team at your side. Those who have joined the ranks of The 2% Club have settled on this smart approach by utilizing the following tips.

Tips for developing investment outside your business

1. Choose a strategy that fits *you*, don't fit yourself to a strategy
2. Seek a client-driven investment model
3. Practice simple investing
4. Look for an advisor who provides transparency and clearly explains all fees

1. Choose a strategy that fits you, don't fit yourself to a strategy

Members of The 2% Club routinely look for an advisor that can help them find and achieve an appropriate strategy. They are not square pegs that try again and again to force themselves into round holes left by cookie-cutter management teams. Investors often feel that they're powerless when it comes to their money and their money manager, and succumbing to this dangerous inertia is ultimately deleterious. You may get lucky and avoid disaster, but when speculating on stocks or timing the market, you're not relying on strategy at that point, you're just closing your eyes and hoping for a lucky break. It's a far better thing to find a manager who understands you and shapes your investment strategy to suit your unique needs. Your advisor needs to take that responsibility seriously, just as you do. If you're paying someone who is in the business of caring about your money, you'd better make sure that *your* investment philosophy matches theirs before you ask them to join you in managing your money.

It's tempting to let your emotions run this decision-making process, and understandably so. When you're talking about the livelihood of your family and the long-term health of your business and/or the cash that you've accumulated from that business, emotions are bound to run high. But you cannot fall victim to the temptation to allow emotions to dictate who you choose to be your financial advisor. Your running buddy or your brother-in-law may be a wonderful confidante, friend, and pace-keeper. However, even if they have the proper certification and connections, that doesn't mean they're going to be the *best* financial advisor for you. The 2% Club choose advisors for their expertise in helping them select appropriate funds to invest in, to minimize taxation (which is one of the biggest expenses of any investment) to help them successfully plan and execute the eventual exit from their business and for their general expertise in helping them make smart financial decisions in a broad range of financial related topics. After all, financial advising is the role of the financial advisor.

This caveat about making emotional decisions goes for the market itself. Often, people will follow emotion-based advice from trusted sources (that same brother-in-law, say) telling them a hot stock is a "sure winner." Panic and fear can also be powerful drivers for investors. The 2% Club know that investing is not about specu-lating or timing the market; they know that the key to a successful investment experience is to buy and hold the right funds for a long period of time. A good investment plan will make all the guesswork unnecessary. Finally, The 2% Club avoids mixing their business life and their personal life, and so should you.

2. Seek a client-driven investment model

One of the unfortunate truths of the financial services industry is that the client isn't always at the center of an advisor's universe. In fact, when I first started out, one of my mentors made this undesirable truth clear to me. When I made the transition from CPA to financial advisor, I sought the counsel of John Bowen, a top coach and mentor in the industry.

John told me that the industry could be most accurately described as *firm-driven*. A firm-driven approach meant that the large investment firms were the ones doing all the research on financial markets and investments, which was then passed down to the smaller fish within the firm (the advisors, like John), which was then passed on to the client. They were selling advice that was meant, on its surface, to be impartial, but was really driven by the firm's own interests and own products. John found that, under this approach, which was the prevailing reality of the time, he felt less like someone who was paid to help people and more like someone who was a glorified salesman, meant to push the company at the expense of the client. The client often had no idea this was going on—and we're not talking fraud here, we're just talking the unfortunate politics of sales-oriented motives. On the contrary, the client was coming to John with their arms (and their portfolios, and their wallets) wide open, totally unable to parse the difficult landscape of the market for themselves and entrusting their funds and their family's future to him.

Needless to say, John didn't feel too good about this.

At night, he'd slip out of his office and into the cushy confines of academia, teaching investment theory at a graduate school at night. While he was doing well at the firm by day, it was the teaching that was really stoking his fire. He enjoyed being able to give truly impartial information, and to truly help people with no ulterior motive—qualities that I shared and admired. What he had been hoping for in the industry he was instead finding in teaching—the school that was writing his paycheck was writing it because they wanted him to be an impartial expert, not because they wanted him to shill their wares, their theories, to the students. Another light-bulb moment came to him when, as he was explaining the firm-driven model that dominated the field in those days, one of his students asked him if this was the method that he used on his own clients.

John told me that, to him, it felt like an eternity before he could answer the question, but it was more likely that he was sucked into a wormhole of introspection about something he'd already been doing a great deal of thinking about. He took a deep breath and admitted to him that, no, he wasn't. What John was trying to impart was a *client-driven* model, where the client was in charge, and he was answerable to him or her.

This story is one of the reasons that I continued to learn from John as a mentor—I recognized that he was a leader in the client-driven model, and I knew in my very core that I agreed with him and believed in his approach. With his help, I knew I could incorporate a client-driven wealth management model within my firm based on the foundations of wealth management that he was promoting.

My firm has always used the client-driven approach, something I take great pride in today. The theories that I preach are the same ones I practice. Under the client-driven model, the clients are at the top, just above the financial advisor. The role of the financial advisor is then to support their clients' needs and goals.

So what is the role of a client-driven advisor? Other than maintaining a deeper relationship than what is seen in firm-driven models, the client-driven financial advisor has two primary responsibilities:

1. The advisor is there to develop a client-appropriate investment strategy, and then implement that strategy by selecting appropriate funds.

2. The advisor has financial expertise in helping solve the financial challenges of a specific type of client, a specialization.

The 2% Club recognizes that advisors are not the same thing as money managers. The investment funds selected by the advisor will have money managers who manage the money in the fund. Those managers' jobs are to execute the strategy of the fund, buying and selling stocks or bonds accordingly. The advisor's job is to consider all factors of a client's situation and select funds with strategies that will achieve the client's specific goals.

Additionally, The 2% Club demands a comprehensive approach from their financial advisors, a specialization that benefits them specifically. Their advisors are responsive to their need to lay the groundwork for a desirable impact on their overall bottom line. A well-chosen small business owner advisor will hold expertise in business valuation, succession planning, and estate protection. These are all critical underpinnings of a successful journey in joining The 2% Club. Not at all coincidentally, these advisors to The 2% Club are knowledgeable about tax issues, since taxes are one of the biggest expenses of successful investing, and even more importantly, tax returns are the single most important document relied on in business valuation and sale, so it matters that it is presented in a way that supports their goals and vision of success. Having a good tax strategy in place is also crucial to making sure that money is not left on the table where capital gains and investments are concerned.

Ultimately, these advisors serve a niche market, small business owners, unlike your average big-firm financial advisor who typically has few business owners on his client list. The focus of these niche advisors on the needs of Main Street business owners has earned them the reputation and the ability to serve an elite cadre of investors.

3. Practice simple investing

Another thing I've learned from my years in the business is that investing has changed. Now, previously complicated investment vehicles have been streamlined, making simpler investing available to those who want to practice it. As you may have guessed, The 2% Club is among the ranks of these investors for whom simplicity is a siren's song.

The 2% Club knows better than to think that the more convoluted a product is, the better it is. Elegance and simplicity don't just apply to design principles for computers and furniture, but in finance and strategy as well. Now, and particularly since about year 2000, investors can benefit from these changes by buying funds that represent diversified microcosms of the market, essentially allowing you to buy an entire market in a single fund.

It's computer automation that we can thank for this. Of the 17,000 stocks in the market, the majority that are worth owning are represented in the 3,340 stocks of the Vanguard Total Stock Market Fund. It accounts for a representative share of 99.5% of the value of the entire stock market. Due to computer automation, fees have been driven down in response to this simplicity, making it possible to own a diversified portfolio within one fund. This simplicity saves time and agony over "strategy" that resembles a dartboard—spreading assets and weakening them over multiple mutual funds or multiple advisors. In this case, diversification doesn't necessarily mean spreading the assets themselves around, it just means taking advantage of changes in investing that allow you to hold diversified positions inexpensively, returning more of the rewards to your portfolio.

Although we're keeping it simple here, there is *one* distinction that is supremely important to make. And that is that you'll need to make sure that your advisor is not both the custodian of your funds and the broker of those funds. One such man who will forever live in infamy is Bernie Madoff—and I don't think I need to sell you on why it's important that you avoid that kind of situation.

4. Look for an advisor who provides transparency and clearly explains all fees

Much like the warnings that I gave about Madoff and knowing who your advisor really works for, it's important that you select an advisor that practices transparency. If you call and ask where your money is, there should be no hesitation in his response. If you want to see an itemized statement of the funds, it should be on your desk within the business day. Your calls should be answered promptly, your questions should be answered promptly, and if you don't understand something and ask for an explanation, that explanation should be delivered promptly and without equivocation.

The same goes for the issue of fees. There are essentially three kinds of fees. Financial advisors charge fees, the funds that are invested in have fees, and there are trade fees for the buying and selling of funds. All of these fees are either hidden or transparent. If you cannot see the fees, it does not mean there are none, it means they are hidden. Would you allow someone to reach into your bank account and just take whatever fee they want without your understanding or even seeing it? Two-percent Club members don't like hidden fees—they want all three kinds of these fees to be transparent.

There are costs to investing; it's just another truism of the market. However, not all costs are the same, and not all costs are reasonable. Make sure that your advisor walks you through the fee structure and what they receive. Are you satisfied with the financial advising you are paying for from your financial advisor? Are they a fee-only advisor whose fees are always transparent, or are they product salesmen who are getting paid from hidden fees for selling you financial products, like the firm-driven advisors of yore? The right financial advisor will help you minimize fees allowing more of the income to be returned for investing.

••••

Once you've used these tips and developed 80% of your wealth outside of your business, you'll have a truly secure position, one that will help you provide for yourself and your loved ones in the future. At this point, it is only a matter of time before complete

Step Eight of the roadmap, a personal budget less than 5% of your net worth, that is, if you haven't achieved it already. A very enviable position, a position that will allow you to retire on your terms, and sell when you're ready to sell, rather than one that keeps you beholden to the uncertainties of a singular market.

After all is said and done and this strategy is put in place, you'll truly have that sense of financial independence that allows you to self-actualize, reaching your full potential.

WORKSHEET:
Develop Investments Outside Your Business

1. Do you have a goal for developing investments outside your business?

2. Do you know the value of your business as a gauge for determining the amount of investments that must be made to achieve the goal of having them represent 80% of your wealth?

3. Have you purchased investment real estate for your portfolio?

4. Have you established a non-tax-deferred brokerage account and begun investing?

5. What financial advising does your financial advisor provide? How did you select them?

6. Is your advisor operating in a firm-driven or client-driven model?

7. What specialized expertise does your financial advisor bring to your relationship that benefits your bottom line?

8. What strategy does your financial advisor employ with regard to your investments? Do you understand that strategy?

9. How does the performance of your investments compare to the performance of the S&P?

10. If you have more than seven mutual funds, why would you pay more in fees and have less diversification than you could with less than three funds?

11. Can you increase your diversification, reduce risk and fees, and improve performance by owning fewer funds?

12. Have you established the financial security and wealth your family and employees expect from you?

RULE FOUR:

RULE FOUR:

Stay Informed About Exit & Succession Planning

You've come a long way down the path to The 2% Club. The focus of this chapter is the ninth step on the roadmap, in fact—you've spent years nurturing a successful business, reining in your personal budget, establishing assets and wealth outside of your business, and being smart about opportunities to expand your revenue while keeping your costs at a minimum. Now, we're ready to start talking about exit and succession planning.

Naturally, there might be some resistance at the thought of selling the business you've worked so hard to build. And that's normal. If you're cut from the same cloth as the entrepreneurs in The 2% Club, you're motivated by this kind of success. Something made you stand up long ago and say that you were going to make your own path, draw your own map, and stop playing into the cycle of employment—being an entrepreneur is in your blood and you were compelled to follow your passion.

But one of the major themes of this book has been thinking ahead. It's not about making decisions based on a fear of the worst-case scenario, it's about taking that legendary vision that you have developed as a successful businessperson and applying it to some of these possible outcomes. The point is to create your best outcome, to stay one step ahead of those dreadful uncertainties when you can, and minimize the damage when you can't.

If you have completed the first eight steps we've talked about, then you know how much hard work you've had to put in to get to this point. Even if you haven't, and you're reading ahead to see what challenges will lie before you, you can see now that planning a successful exit can and should start as early as when you open the business—looking forward and building value before volume. You can sell your business at any point to complete this ninth step, but if you haven't completed the first eight, you are most likely (though not always) leaving your business as a part of the 98%—not The 2% Club. So if you want to join those ranks, my advice to you is to stay farsighted, and begin with the end in mind.

Ultimately, if you truly care about your business, you care about its legacy. And if you truly care about your financial well-being not just in the *now*, but in the *years from now*, you will see that following the Fourth Rule of The 2% Club, by staying informed about exit and succession planning, will help you be effective in creating your best outcome and greatly improving your bottom line.

••••

Now that we've established that you're always ready to be thinking about this—even if you're not ready to act on it—let's dive right in to this game-changing strategy. Once you've developed 80% of your wealth outside your business as we discussed in Rule Three, exit and succession planning may start to seem much more real to you. Even if you haven't developed 80% of your wealth outside your business, you may have started to realize that, with the sale of your business, you can become financially independent. That is the ultimate goal for many business owners: not just to see something they've built rise to become a success, but to be able to retire on that asset (mixed with a responsibly allocated portfolio, of course)—or maybe move on to something else. This forward thinking is precisely what those members of The 2% Club have been looking towards when they started to develop wealth and investment-related income streams outside of their business— so that when they *were* ready to hand over the reins, it would be financially feasible. If you've successfully developed 80% of your wealth outside your business, you're ready for the next part.

••••

Write Your Own Ending:
To whom, when, and for how much will you sell?

As we discussed in Rule One at the beginning of the book, understanding business valuation is crucial if you hope to be in this for the long haul. If you want to make sure that the Emperor isn't walking around in the nude, you're going to have to use reliable, realistic projections, tax returns, cash flow, and other value drivers to be able to *display* that your business is worth what you say it is. This is how you'll earn clout and collateral as you move along, gaining market share and preparing your business for its ultimate purpose—part of the plan to care for yourself and your loved ones in the years to come.

The same philosophy comes into play for Rule Four. Essentially, The 2% Club (and therefore, you should too!) views this as understanding business valuation in a planning context. This means that everything you do to implement an exit plan capitalizes on everything that makes your business more valuable, again, thinking for the longer term. Problems that are addressed now and molded to realign your business to your exit plan can be turned into assets when it comes time for the sale phase, whereas problems ignored can fester and grow.

So what could some of this planning look like? For example, one of the valuable benefits of your business is your employees and their collective knowledge base, taking this into account while exit planning may mean that you lock down some of those key employees contractually or with incentive programs to get them to stay through the transition or sale. This sort of tactic must be executed well in advance of a sale. Or, if one of the key factors of your exit plan is the size of the business and the slice of market share, in order to make sure that it continues into the sale, you may put a management team in place to help grow the business to the point where you can get to larger multiples (and more profit) when it comes time to sell. Or you may look at your exit plan and decide that you need to take things down to brass tacks, improving your marketability and cash flow to achieve the value that you'd like to see come out of the sale. Whatever your strategy is, you'll take the tool of business valuation in a planning context and use it to project for the value you'd like to see, and then plan to achieve that value.

When you consider your exit or succession plan, you'll need to keep three key questions in mind:

> ❯ To *whom* do you want to sell?
> ❯ For *how much* do you want to sell?
> ❯ *When* do you want to sell?

Like other aspects of planning discussed in this book, unlocking the answers to these questions can frequently be accomplished through your business valuation. A credible valuation will serve as fodder for planning a strategy around how to get to where you want to go. If you discover that you want to sell by a certain date, you will need to adjust your planning to get your valuation in line by that certain date. If you want to sell to a certain type of buyer, you might need to adjust your strategy so that your valuation reflects a business that such a buyer would want to buy. And on it goes. It may seem circuitous, but all good outcomes have at their base a good foundation—one built on strategy. When you've answered these three key questions, you truly understand the ending that you want to write—and what it will take to get there.

Exit Options *(To whom do you want to sell?)*

When looking at those three questions, the answer to the first question is something that you will choose from a set of predetermined options. If the end you have in mind is one that sees your business transferring to a family member, for example, you'll build your strategy accordingly.

There are essentially eight options for exiting your business. One thing to keep in mind as you read about these options is that Main Street businesses—the category into which most of you will fall—have a more restrictive set of options than middle-market, larger-cap businesses. It's a matter of practicality. Although there are eight exit options, the first four are the most practical for Main Street businesses to implement, the others will likely cost you way more than they are worth.

1. **Liquidation**—you close your business and sell the assets; an option frequently used by the other 98%.
2. **Sale to Insider**—someone in your company, an employee or co-owner.
3. **Sale to Third Party**—a vendor, competitor, or independent buyer.
4. **Transfer to Family Member**—50% of owners want to do this but less than one-third are successful.
5. **ESOP/MBO**—employee stock option program/ management buy-out.

6. **Private Company Recapitalization**—a substantial portion of ownership (say, 80%) is sold to a larger company, and you as the current owner retain a smaller share (say, 20%). This way, you retain a job, and you have the benefits of a liquidation event.

7. **Private Equity Group Sale**—sophisticated buyers that you'll most commonly find buying a business in the middle-market and not on Main Street.

8. **Initial Public Offering**—or "going public" in the stock market.

Options five through eight are mainly for the middle market, not Main Street. And you don't want to be lumped in with many in the 98% that are forced to choose option one. Most successful Main Street businesses will end up selling to an insider, a third party, or transferring to a family member.

Positioning Through Planning (*For how much and when do you want to sell?*)

After you've determined how (and to whom) you want to sell your business, you will need to go back to business valuation to project what sort of value you might get in a sale. Once you understand your current situation, you can use your valuation to develop strategy to better position yourself—either for the amount or for the target date that you desire.

To really grasp this part of the strategy, it's important to understand how trends can affect the value of your business. Think of a chart depicting the rise and fall of the Dow Jones Industrial Average. This is one of the more familiar forms that trends take on—one that's plastered all over the financial news and your portfolio statements. Small business values go up and down just like the stock of businesses in the Dow and vice versa. Just like the stocks on this chart, your business has downward and upward trends—but because your business is much smaller, it's a much more risky and more volatile stock. This is why preparation for all eventualities (or as many as you can reasonably prepare for) is so crucial if you wish to join The 2% Club. They understand that the value of their business isn't a fixed point, but rather a fluctuating range of values that may not always be favorable.

Learning how to read these trends is very important. Were I to look at your business as a valuation analyst, I would look at the most recent historical record—much as we would have done with your initial valuation—using the past three years or so of documentation (tax returns and the like) to project the future earnings of your company. Since we've noted that three to five years of historical performance will be used for valuation at the time of sale closing, these are the three to five years that are most meaningful to the valuation of your business at sale—and careful attention to the story their trend tells is very important.

Obviously, we'd like to see that trend going in a stable, upwards trajectory. If this is indeed the case, you are in a better position to get the amount you'd prefer to receive in the sale. This is not only because your buyers will want to buy it, but because any banks involved in financing the deal will agree to the financing. Small businesses are stocks just like those in the stock market, people love to buy them when they are going up and are running scared when they are going down. The financing—mostly in the form of bank issued, SBA guaranteed loans for the types of Main Street businesses we're talking about—is based on the projected future cash flow of the business. So you see, when you are selling a business, you are selling future cash flows. When you buy a business, you are buying future cash flows. Since most small businesses buyers borrow all the money they can to purchase the business, the value is essentially limited to debt that the projected cash flow can support, assuming a 10-25% equity infusion from the buyer.

Sometimes a seller or buyer will suggest a seller-financed sale on contract. Unless there is a crisis where the seller cannot continue with the business, this will rarely make sense. Essentially, the seller is giving the buyer their cash flow and the buyer is giving it back. Sellers will say, "Why would I do that? I could just keep the business and the cash flow, and in the future, at the point where the contract would have been satisfied, I will have all the same cash flow and still own the business."

This is true. The thing that is in it for the seller when selling a business is that they get paid future cash flow today and shift the risk to the buyer of whether or not that cash flow materializes in future periods.

Now we must return to the story your tax returns tell. If your valuation uncovers a downward trend, it's obviously not cause for celebration. Even though everyone knows that business values go up and down like the stock market, it's very difficult to sell a business with projections that go the wrong way. Even though you can spin it—and reasonably so—by saying that the market will pick up again, it's difficult to convince a buyer to buy, or a bank to bank the deal when there are downward trends.

But the trend of your projections isn't the only moving target that you're going to have to come to understand. Just like you would find for a used car, your business has different values for different buyers. A used car's value goes up a bit from a car lot trade-in, to a private sale, to a sale made by a dealer on his lot, and that's because buyers have a different level of comfort and leverage in each of those situations. The same goes for your business. You might sell it for less if you're selling it to a family member than if you're in a position to sell it to a competitor salivating over the chance to take over your share of the market.

It all circles back to our three questions: to whom do you want to sell it, what price do you want to sell it for, and when do you want to sell? Interestingly, you will most likely only have control over a couple of these answers. If your focused on getting the a particular increase in value, you should sell when your business achieves that value and the conditions are right—but that gives you less control over the date. If you pick a certain date where you'd like to offload the business, that will give you control over the timing, but leaves you powerless when it comes to deciding the value, as those values are volatile.

Consider one case study, a sixty-six-year-old construction-related business owner we'll call Paul. Paul is now resting comfortably in the halls of The 2% Club, having worked hard *and* smart. Before the sale of his construction business, Paul had real estate worth $700,000, bonds worth $500,000, and stocks worth $1,000,000. His business had a value of $2.3 million before he was ready to sell. In 2008, when he was about to sell, he earned a profit of just over $500,000. So, Paul was doing pretty well for himself, having a diversified portfolio of assets outside of his business, although his business was doing well in its own right.

Like his counterparts in The 2% Club, Paul didn't let his largesse get to him. He kept his living expenses low, living only on $120,000 per year even when his income was climbing up to half a million. He hung on to the business through an upward trend in the real estate market, riding the boom. He had a figure in mind: He wanted to retire when his business was worth $2 million, leaving enough for him to live on and some for emergencies for the rest of his life. Because he had not accumulated 80% of his wealth outside of his business, we knew that it was important for him to focus on selling when his business was worth $2 million, rather than picking a specific date to sell. Once the business went to $2 million, he was prepared, and was able to put it up for sale and sell it very quickly.

As we all know, Paul's story could have turned out very differently, the real estate market crashed shortly thereafter and so did the value of his construction business. Had he focused on a date rather than a value, he would likely still be working today, some five years later.

Again, the more dependent you are on the proceeds from the sale of your business to achieve your financial goals, the less control you will have over the date you sell. If this is the case for you, then you should consider a range of dates, perhaps a five-year window, within which you are prepared to sell when conditions are all green and your business will fetch the value you need.

Let's look at another case study—one where my firm was able to help the business owner understand these trends and practice what we call a value enhancement process—where we see what's in front of us and look ahead to see where we want to be, then bridge the gap between those two places. In this case, we were dealing with a Main Street business in video production. In July of 2011, the company came to our firm to get a business valuation—they had a distressed co-owner in their midst (one of the dreaded D's: divorce) and the partners needed to organize a buy-out.

The SBA business valuation we conducted concluded that the business was worth $472,000. After buying out his distressed co-owner, the owner returned to us interested in exit planning for the purposes of eventually selling to an employee. He needed to get net proceeds of $500,000 out of the sale; this would allow him to exit the business and meet his financial goals. With the business being worth only $472,000, the owner would need to sell it for nearly $700,000 to walk away after paying taxes with the $500,000 net he wanted.

Our firm analyzed the situation and found that the company needed to do two things to enhance its value. First, they needed to improve the credible, tax return-verifiable cash flow. Second, they needed to develop a company packed with buyer benefit statements. We gave our findings to the owner, together with information on value and volume and had him get to work. As evidenced in this case, entrepreneurs can be extremely resourceful people when they fully understand the task at hand.

In less than two years, the company more than doubled its cash flow, resulting in an updated SBA valuation of over $1 million. The value drivers were bulked up, putting in place a heavily stacked buyer benefit statement. Currently, as a result of the work that they've done, the company has two full-price competing purchase offers to choose from.

That's not a bad place to be.

••••

For your convenience, I've gathered the following tips to summarize what we've just gone over.

Tips for Exit Planning

1. Buyer benefit statements are business value drivers.
2. Plan for a financial sale.
3. You can pick your value or you can pick your date, but not both.
4. Position your investments in advance.
5. Not selling your business *is* an option, but you still need an exit plan.

1. Buyer benefit statements are business value drivers

Visualize that it's a number of years down the road and you have decided to sell your business. Sit down and make a list of all of the attractive characteristics that you have built into your business that will have great value to a buyer. It might look something like this:

- The business practically runs itself; your employees are well trained, efficient and capable.
- You have focused on profit, not size; in so doing, you have developed great value for your customer and have a product that's different with limited competition.
- You have organized your business in a way that minimizes taxes for the new owner.
- Your processes are organized and blueprinted, making it easy for a new owner to step in and be successful.

- The employees are on incentive plans that make it attractive for them to stay with the new owner and help the new owner be a success.
- You have a long-standing good name and reputation in the community.

As you can see, the things that make your business more valuable also make your business a better one for you to own. The point where you want to sell the business the least (because of how well it is going), is probably also the point where it is worth the most and will sell for its highest value.

2. Plan for a financial sale

A Main Street business is one with less than $10 million of annual sales. Main Street businesses with less than $3 million of annual sales account for 90% of all United States businesses, and they have an average market value of $750,000. A strategic value is one where the investment value to the buyer for purchasing a business greatly exceeds the financial value. A financial value is determined based on the free cash flow a business generates, and the value is essentially the same as the amount of debt that the free cash flow could support, after accounting for a 10-25% equity infusion on behalf of the buyer. It is extremely rare for a Main Street business to sell for a strategic value. Most Main Street businesses will sell for a financial value. Most will be financed with a loan guaranteed by the SBA. While buyer benefit statements make a Main Street business more saleable, the limiting factor for business value (for Main Street businesses) is generally free cash flow.

3. You can pick your value or you can pick your date, but not both

It's really nice to think that you could sell your business on the date that you want to, to the person you want to, and for the amount of money that you want. But the truth is that you can pick your value or you can pick your date, but you can't pick both. The more dependent you are on the proceeds from the sale of your business, the less control over the date you will have.

Consider that back at the end of 2008 and the beginning of 2009, the largest companies in the United States lost over 50% of their value in a span of just six months. Smaller companies can be even *more* volatile and risky. Your small company could easily lose over 50% of its value in a span of six months, or, it could more than double its value in a span of six months.

The 2% Club who have invested more than 80% of their wealth outside their business, control the date they sell. They control the date because they are not dependent on the proceeds from their business for their lifestyle and retirement, allowing them to take whatever value is there on the date they want to leave.

The more dependent you are on the proceeds from your business for your lifestyle and retirement, the less control over the date you will have. You will need to focus on selling your business when the value you need arrives and the conditions for sale are good. If you are in this situation, I recommend you have a range of dates in mind and sell your business when the value is there.

4. Position your investments in advance

A good financial plan, which is what an exit plan truly is, will coordinate your investments and taxes together with the planned sale of your business and can add tremendously to your bottom line. Look for an advisor who specializes in Main Street businesses and has the expertise to coordinate this sort of planning years in advance. This advisor won't see unrelated bits of information; they will see opportunities to greatly enhance your wealth by coordinating all the moving pieces of your financial plan while helping you execute the Five Rules of The 2% Club.

5. Not selling your business *is* an option, but you still need an exit plan

I guarantee you that one day, whether you want to or not, you will exit your business. In our next chapter, I am going to discuss options for contingency planning. More than 50% of the business owners I have met tell me that they don't plan to sell their business; that they want to work indefinitely, but simply want a plan in case something happens. While I consider exit planning, like we've discussed in this chapter, to be an offensive game plan, contingency planning is an invaluable defensive game plan that every 2% Club hopeful should have.

WORKSHEET:
Stay Informed About Exit & Succession Planning

1. Visualize that it's years down the road and you are ready to sell your business. What are some of the benefits you have created in your business that will have value to the buyer you intend to sell to? Have you built your business to be able to sell it?

2. What has to happen between now and the time that I plan to sell my business to create benefit statements that will make my business attractive to a buyer?

3. Have I put in place incentive plans for key employees where part of the award is paid out in future periods to create an incentive for them to stay through any ownership transition?

4. What value do you think you will need to be able to sell your business? What value is your business worth now? Do you understand the gap and what will have to happen in future periods to close the gap and successfully sell your business so you can retire?

5. What date do you want to sell your business? Will you be able to accumulate 80% of your wealth outside

your business so that you can control the date, or will you need to focus on the value and retire when circumstances allow it?

6. Who do you want to sell it to? How would you like that sale to look, in your ideal world?

7. Do you intend to continue working in the business after the sale? If so, have you considered writing your job description for after the sale so that the buyer can see what you intend to be available to do?

8. What if none of your ideal scenarios are available? Can you still get by, financially?

Protect Your Assets

Any good strategy has offensive and defensive measures. At this point in our journey together, it should come as no surprise to you that I highly recommend those defensive measures! While a good 2% Club candidate never ignores one at the expense of the other, those defensive measures are essential to make sure that the financial house you've worked so hard to build stays safe and in order.

In the last chapter, we discussed the importance of planning as a framework for a successful exit from your business, no matter what form that might take for you. This chapter is also about planning, though, unfortunately, the inevitabilities you're planning for aren't necessarily so sunny. You might feel a little discouraged, reading about all the doom and gloom, and that's normal. I can guarantee you even the best of The 2% Club members probably felt the same thing when they were going over their defensive planning. But the thing that separates them from the rest of the crowd is that they are able to continue to comfortably reap the benefits of their hard work without worrying about all the things they can't control. They're high-wire artists who practice with a net. It doesn't make them less brave, it just makes them smarter.

The 2% Club exercises these defensive tips:

Tips for Protecting Your Wealth

1. Understand the role of insurance
2. Understand your appetite for risk-taking
3. Create a contingency plan
4. Create an estate plan following the three P's
5. Protect yourself against theft

1. Understand the role of insurance

Throughout the lifetime of your company, and hopefully at its inception, you've met with legal experts and tax professionals and done the due diligence to ensure that you're set up properly and all your paperwork is above board. Still, legal issues crop up, and lawsuits can happen. And there's only so much you can do to protect your wealth by legal means. When those methods fail—or become unavailable—you will need yet another backup plan, a surge protector of sorts for your business.

Protecting your wealth is all about risk management. So is the insurance industry. Often times, clients will come to me and ask about those aforementioned legal means to wealth protection. They wonder if they should keep their assets in a trust, set up multiple corporations, and so on. But ultimately, all those legal means will never be bullet proof. A good insurance policy is truly your last line of defense, and maintaining this policy is the smart thing to do; it's what The 2% Club does, certainly.

More than having adequate protection, The 2% Club tends to conduct its business in a way that doesn't leave them open to a lot of liability. So that's the first thing, and it's a foundational issue not to be taken lightly. I can happily say that guiding my clients through a legal morass is something that I haven't had to do, mostly because of this fact. But if they were to run into trouble, The 2% Club absolutely carries proper insurance. If you're worried about whether or not you have enough insurance, you should meet with your insurance advisor annually to assure that your business activities are covered. On the personal side, the same holds true. Additionally, a good umbrella policy is added protection well worthwhile. All umbrella policy insurers will absolutely require that everything underneath that umbrella is effectively insured, ensuring that you're properly protected.

2. Understand your appetite for risk-taking

In my observations of The 2% Club, I've found that they all share certain defensive measures or protective concerns in common. The first step they'll take is to clearly evaluate their entrepreneurial appetite for risk.

Entrepreneurs didn't hone their entrepreneurial spirit by playing it safe. It stands to reason, then, that after some entrepreneurs have successfully sold and exited from their business, they'd like to use some of that now-liquid capital to get back in the game. I had one client who had sold his company, walking away with a net of $3 million. While we were taking him through the sale, he had told us he was planning to retire and live on the proceeds of the sale, doing some occasional, low-risk consulting work from time to time. But his entrepreneurial spirit wasn't so easily squelched. About six months later, he came back to us and told us he was thinking of taking his $3 million and putting it back into another startup venture.

Every client is different, and outcomes always vary. But in this case, I had to advise against sinking the *entire* $3 million back into the startup phase. Here was a client who had already successfully gone through the steps to joining The 2% Club, and was looking to start over again from the beginning. Only now, his circumstances had changed. He was older, with more responsibilities and less earning years in front of him. What would happen to his family while he was dumped back into the mostly famine feast-or-famine roulette of the startup phase? What if he got sick and needed to pay hospital bills, or was unable to put in the time that was required of the rigorous process of starting up a business? And what were the odds that he would be able to rejoin The 2% Club again at the end of it all?

The odds are—you guessed it—about 2%.

Another client found this out the hard way when he sunk his entire sale proceeds into a real estate venture at the wrong time. When the markets imploded in 2008, he went bankrupt—all because he'd failed to heed the same advice that got him to the top in the first place, and had put too much of his assets at risk. The

2% Club, in this situation, wouldn't have put any more than 20% of their assets into the new venture—in which case, in the instance of catastrophic failure, they're not so bad off. The same can't be said of this client, unfortunately, who put himself in the position of having to try to recover from bankruptcy at age sixty, which is no easy feat.

But the breaks don't always have to be so rough. If you can engage in a little self-reflection and override your entrepreneurial appetite for risk, you will find that staying business savvy doesn't mean you have to hang up your hat for good. Mac's is one success story I always return to when I'm warning entrepreneurs about re-exposing themselves to these types of risks. Unlike our last two tales, this one has a happy ending.

Mac is a 2% Club member who made his fortune in the rare coins and precious metals business. He worked hard, lived well within his means, and had amassed a personal net worth of $3 million outside of his business. When it came time to sell his business, he was able to sell it for $1 million, bringing his assets up to $4 million. He was now ready to walk away from the daily grind, but not away from his entrepreneurial spirit.

He had built a small cabin by a peaceful lake where he liked to go on his vacations. His plan was to take 10% of his $4 million and build a shop with all the right equipment right there on his property where he could manufacture barbecues on a small scale— a hobby of his that he wanted to turn into a small business to keep him busy during retirement. Instead of going all in and losing it all, Mac was able to satisfy his entrepreneurial appetite while still maintaining his safety net.

3. Create a contingency plan

A rather self-explanatory but often-overlooked aspect of defensive strategy is to make sure that you have a contingency plan in place. This is different from exit planning, to a certain extent, keeping in mind that, whether we like it or not, we're all going to exit our business at one time, and not always in a clean-cut sale. Sometimes, unfortunately, there are more emergent situations that arise.

In this case, you'll need to have a plan that assures continuity of your business and assets in the event that you're no longer alive or able to run your business. Take the time to get down on paper all your important paswords, bank account access codes, and a clear-cut plan for who should continue your duties in your absence. You should also think about the different buy-sell scenarios that you might want to have triggered upon the occurrence of certain events, and put in place a buy-sell agreement if possible.

4. Create an estate plan following the three P's

When it comes to estate planning, many people incorrectly assume that the biggest issue to contend with is tax-related. In fact, this is far from the truth. While specific laws change over time, the reality of the estate tax exemption is that the limits are usually higher than most people's estates, particularly Main Street business owners as opposed to the middle-market kingpins. Usually, the questions of process are the bolded items at the top of the list when it comes to estate planning.

I tell clients that an effective estate plan focuses on the three P's:

- What **Property** do you have?
- What **People** do you want to give it to?
- What **Process** do we use to make that happen?

As a starting point, having appropriately-executed legal documents like a will, healthcare directives, and powers of attorney in place will be necessary. The next step will be to make sure that all of the documentation on each account—each savings, retirement, investment portfolio and so on—lines up with those wills and directives. A simple example is making sure the beneficiary designations on your investment accounts are in line with what you state in your will, because the beneficiary statements will be followed regardless of what your will instructs. Each type of asset uses a different process to transfer, and having everything correctly lined up in this way can mean the difference between your property falling through a legal loophole and being properly transferred in accordance with your actual wishes.

5. Protect yourself against theft

The final, and potentially most unpleasant, area of vulnerability to address is one that nobody likes to think about. But as our case studies have proven, avoidance isn't the best strategy for getting ahead. It's an unfortunate truth that, each year, many businesses are significantly impacted by some type of financial fraud perpetrated by a trusted employee.

I've heard it over and over again from business owners: "My bookkeeper can't steal from me; I'm the only one with signature authority on the checking account."

The bad news is that even signature authority can't keep someone with fraudulent intentions at bay. If you're not the one reconciling the bank accounts or policing the money, you're not going to notice the fraud. Even if you are the only one who signs the checks, what's to keep your signature from being forged? If you're not looking at the ledger, you'll be none the wiser.

On the small business level, internal controls simply don't work. I've seen a number of businesses go bankrupt over this issue. The average fraud goes on for about eighteen months before it's discovered, but by that time, it has cost the business hundreds of thousands of dollars. And by the time all is said and done, the money is usually never recuperated.

The good news is that there's a fairly simple solution to this pervasive problem, and it's called prevention. Police your money and assets; look carefully and frequently at what is going on.

Consider reviewing copies of checks to see if they make sense. Do surprise inspections. By keeping an eye on your money and protecting your wealth, if you're unfortunate enough to be the victim of fraud, you can stop the bleeding before it's too late.

WORKSHEET:
Protecting Your Assets

1. Do you have proper business insurance coverage?

2. Do you have a personal umbrella insurance policy?

3. What's your appetite for risk? If you were to sell your business today, would you get back in the game right away? How much money would it be safe for you to use for that purpose?

4. What property do you have, what people do you want it to go to, and will the process that is used to transfer that type of asset work according to the wishes in your will?

5. What measures are you currently taking to protect yourself from theft? Are you doing more than internal control by inspecting your assets?

CHAPTER 5

Creating Your Plan

Much of what we've talked about in this book has had to do with the future: predictions, positioning, setting goals, and being able to visualize a future in which you are successful, in which your future in The 2% Club is clearly visible. To this end, it is helpful to have a plan, something simple, effective, and written.

Few business owners I know have a detailed, written, business plan. Even fewer have a written personal financial plan, much less one that is connected to their business. They may have had a plan at one time, but plans become outdated quickly, and as each day passes, circumstances change, making it difficult to keep current. The practical solution is to create a plan with a very short, but routinely updated, set of goals based on a long-term vision and short-term actions. To help you create your plan for joining The 2% Club, I have included some worksheets here that can help you to do just that. Once you have completed the worksheets, you will have created your plan by identifying your long-term vision, understanding which of the 10 Steps you have left to complete, and selecting your most pressing, short-term moves to make.

You should update your plan once a year, making additional updates whenever your business or personal financial goals change significantly. Updating your plan regularly will keep you focused, helping you to make a series of good financial decisions, ones that follow the Five Rules, resulting in your success and membership in The 2% Club.

Creating Your Plan

What are Your Plans for Your Business:

What is your vision for your business between now and the day you exit? Do you plan to sell your business one day or work indefinitely? To whom will you sell, for how much, and when? What conditions would have to exist for you to sell? Lets say it is years down the road and you have sold you business, what are you doing?

What are your personal financial goals / obstacles:

What is your net worth? (fill out net worth stmt below) How much do you think you will need for retirement?

1.

2.

3.

Income Worksheet		
Your Wages	$	/ yr
Spouse Wages	$	/ yr
Business	$	/ yr
Real Estate	$	/ yr
Investments	$	/ yr
Pensions	$	/ yr
_____	$	/ yr
_____	$	/ yr
Total	$	/ yr

Net Worth Worksheet			
	Value	Owed	Net Worth
Home	$	$	$
Real Estate	$	$	$
Stock Mkt	$	$	$
Business	$	$	$
_____	$	$	$
_____	$	$	$
_____	$	$	$
Totals	$	$	$

Where are you on the 10 Steps of The 2% Club?
Calculate these key metrics to illuminate your next steps.

A) Annual Pre-Tax Household Income?	B) Annual Personal After Tax Budget?	C) Investment Debt Paid Off Annually?	D) How Much Do You Invest Annually Now?
$	$	$	$

E) How Many Years Until You Exit the Business?	F) Personal Budget Times Yrs in Retirement	G) Invested Net Worth (Excluding Home)	H) What is The Current Value of Your Business?
	$	$	$

What is Your Personal Budget as a Percentage of Income? (From Above, B Divided by A) = _____%

Personal Budget as a Percentage of Net Worth? (From Above, B Divided by G) = _____%

What is Your Annual Rate of Investment? (From Above, C Plus D) = $_____

How Much More Will You Invest Before You Exit? (From Above, (C Plus D) Times E) = $_____

Your Business Value as a Percentage of Your Net Worth? (From Above, H Divided by G) = $_____

Do You Have an Invested Net Worth Gap? (From Above, F Minus G) = $_____

Evaluation

Step 1: Have you established a successful, profitable business?	Yes	No
Step 2: Are you living on < 70% of your household income?	Yes	No
Step 3: Have you established a brokerage account for investments?	Yes	No
Step 4: Have you purchased commercial real estate for your business?	Yes	No
Step 5: Have you paid off your personal residence?	Yes	No
Step 6: Have you achieved a personal budget of < 50% of your income?	Yes	No
Step 7: Have you developed 80% of your wealth outside your business?	Yes	No
Step 8: Have you achieved a personal budget < 3-5% of your net worth?	Yes	No
Step 9: Do you have an exit plan and contingency plan for your business?	Yes	No
Step 10: Welcome to the 2% Club!		

What are the Next Moves in Your Plan? (From Smart Moves Below or Highlight Below)

1.

2.

3.

Some Smart Moves of The 2% Club

Rule 1: Understand Business Valuation:

- ☑ Obtain Certified Business Valuation
- ☑ Read and Understand Your Business Valuation
- ☑ Learn How To Read The Story Your Tax Returns Tell
- ☑ Set Your Business Value Goal, Convert to Profit Goal
- ☑ Create Unique Customer Value Proposition
- ☑ Establish Projections For Targeted Value
- ☑ Increase Volume To Targeted Profit Goal
- ☑ Update Your Business Valuation Annually

Rule 2: Use Tax Strategies That Build Your Wealth:

- ☑ Review Tax Reduction Strategies With Your Advisor
- ☑ Ask Advisor For Tax Strategies That Build Wealth
- ☑ Review The Business Valuation Compensation Analysis
- ☑ Review Compensation Planning To Minimize Taxes
- ☑ Consider Reporting Taxes On Cash Basis Vs. Accrual
- ☑ Purchase Commercial Real Estate For Your Business
- ☑ Tax Loss Harvest In Down Markets To Bank Losses
- ☑ Develop Non-Tax Deferred Assets To Tax Diversify

Rule 3: Develop Investments Outside Your Business:

- ☑ Get Your Personal Budget To <70% of Your Income
- ☑ Pay Off Your Personal Residence and Maintain
- ☑ Get Your Personal Budget to <50% of Your Income
- ☑ Purchase Investment Real Estate
- ☑ Select A Financial Advisor With Valuable Expertise
- ☑ Set a Goal For An Amount of Outside Investments
- ☑ Select An Advisor That Uses a Client-Driven Model
- ☑ Develop 80% of Your Wealth Outside Your Business

Rule 4: Stay Informed About Exit & Succession Planning:

- ☑ Write Your 2% Club Plan & Select Your Next Moves
- ☑ Consider Who, When & How Much To Sell For
- ☑ Lock-in Key Employees With Incentives
- ☑ Write Your Own Post-Sale Job Description
- ☑ Consider Buyer Benefit Statements To Install
- ☑ Should Your Plan Focus On Sale Value or Sale Date
- ☑ Consider Your Ideal Buyer and Backup Plan Buyer
- ☑ Rework Your Plan Annually or In Significant Change

Rule 5: Protect Yourself:

- ☑ Develop A Written Contingency Plan
- ☑ Execute Buy/Sell Agreements When Possible
- ☑ Update Buy/Sell Annually With An Annual Valuation
- ☑ Carry Proper Business & Personal Insurance
- ☑ Obtain An Umbrella Insurance Policy
- ☑ Evaluate Your Property, People & Process
- ☑ Execute Complete Estate Planning Documents
- ☑ Police Your Money And Assets Regularly

CHAPTER 6

Finding "The Missing Advisor"

If you choose to seek out an advisor to work with, I recommend that you visit the web site www.TheMissingAdvsior.com, where I post up-to-date information on how to find qualified advisors whose expertise is Main Street Business Owners. I only list information about advisors and organizations who display competence, professionalism and a commitment to executing the concepts outlined in this book.

A strong word of caution: If you are a Main Street business, regardless of how you find an advisor, you must find an advisor who specializes in Main Street Business Owners.

There are many reasons it is important to select an advisor who specializes in Main Street. The solutions and costs for Middle Market businesses are substantially different than those for Main Street. You will be greatly disappointed with the results if you wind up trying to implement a mismatched solution. The business valuation and value drivers are different, the business sale process is different, tax strategies are different, the ideal buyers are different, and on and on. Shockingly, in spite of the fact that over 90% of all businesses are technically classified as a Main Street business, finding a qualified professional who specializes in Main Street can be quite difficult. You will know when you have found the right one; they will have solutions that are practical and reasonable for you to implement, and it will feel like a good fit. Most of all, the right advisor will be able to illustrate how they can bring value that shows up on your bottom line.

In many cases, an advisor will have assembled a small team to accommodate required expertise they don't posses. Overall, the Main Street advisor team should consist of two or three professionals who collectively posses expertise in exit planning, financial advising, taxation, business valuation, and estate protection. Working together as a team, it can be a powerful combination, one that can create tremendous results in helping you to join The 2% Club.

••••

My mission of becoming "The Missing Advisor" for my clients has always been a very personal one for me. Reaching back to when I was on that doctor's table, hearing the words that everyone fears and no one wants to have to plan for, I've been on the front lines of uncertainty. I've been in the dark. But along the way, I was able to visualize that better future, and I was able to actualize it. I like to think that I've learned as much from my clients—the people you've heard me talk about in the pages of this book—as they've learned from me. If you've found this roadmap to The 2% Club to be useful, if you think it might be *your* path to that better future, I'd encourage you to reach out and search for *your* Missing Advisor.

Best of Success,

Tom Griffiths

Thomas M. Griffiths

CPA, MBA, PFS, ABV, CEPA

OBTAIN A CERTIFIED BUSINESS VALUATION

If you've read this book and you're ready to get started on your journey to The 2% Club, then you'll know that the first step is the completion of a strong, certified business valuation. Griffiths, Dreher and Evans boast decades of experience in offering Main Street business owners precisely the foundation they need to enjoy success for the years to come. Our analysts perform over 100 valuations a year nationwide. We'd love the chance to include you in our growing list of happy clients, and would like to extend a special offer to our main street business owner readers.

For a discounted price of $750 (with proof of purchase of this book), our Certified Business Valuation Analysts will put together an SBA Compliant Business Valuation for your business. Our valuations meet the Uniform Standards of Professional Appraisal Practices and are referred to by AICPA Valuation Standards as a Conclusion of Value.[*]

To qualify for this special offer, your business must have annual revenue of under $10 million per year and you must provide proof of purchase of this book within one year prior to engaging us for the valuation. To take advantage of this offer and jumpstart your journey to The 2% Club, please call 509-326-4054 or email abv@grifco.com.

*This offer is subject to withdrawal and modification, at any time, without further notice.

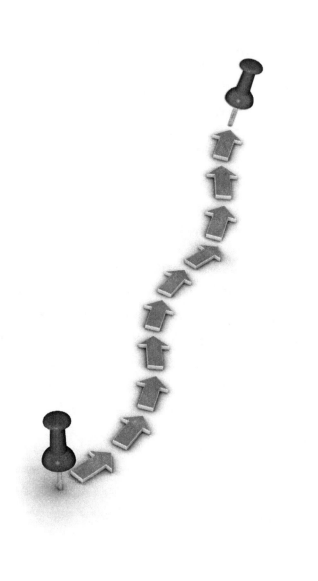

About the author

Thomas M. Griffiths, CPA, MBA ABV, PFS, CEPA is one of the founders and principals of Griffiths, Dreher & Evans, a leading firm combining the expertise of business valuation, investment advisors and certified public accountants. Tom founded the firm in 1992, building it on the philosophy that in order to achieve long-term success, business owners needed advice that transcended what was typically available to them. This emphasis on holistic planning as the bedrock of strategy has helped hundreds of business owners grow and harvest the value of their small businesses.

Tom holds a bachelor's and MBA from Eastern Washington University, as well as a broad range of professional designations in exit planning, financial forensics, and valuation, among others. His ground-breaking research on the five rules of successful business owners—The 2% Club—has appeared in a number of publications and earned him speaking engagements at major national conferences.

He is a veteran of the Air Force National Guard, and lives in Washington with his wife and their two children.

Acknowledgements

I would like to thank all those who participated in life's unpredictable journey that resulted in this book. In particular, I want to thank Brett Smith, Shawn Coleman, Susan Marshall, Deanna Dreher, Todd Evans, and Kelly Klossner—my co-workers, who grant me the privilege of leadership and who experienced so much change and challenge while we re-invented our practice. Thanks to Don Howard, my doctor, who always insisted he would have me 100% again.

CPSIA information can be obtained at www.ICGtesting.com
Printed in the USA
BVOW04*2156301214

381471BV00002B/3/P